CW00591306

More Adventures on Willow Farm

By Enid Blyton

HINKLER
BOOKS

Cover Illustration: Peter Wilks, sga Illustration & Design, Suffolk, UK
Illustrations: Peter Wilks, sga Illustration & Design, Suffolk, UK
Typesetting: Palmer Higgs, Box Hill, Victoria, Australia

More Adventures on Willow Farm
First published in 1943 by Country Life
This edition published in 2004 by Hinkler Books Pty Ltd
17–23 Redwood Drive
Dingley VIC 3172 Australia
www.hinklerbooks.com

ISBN 1 7412 1433 5

Printed and bound in Australia

The Author
Enid Blyton

Enid Blyton is one of the best-loved writers of the twentieth century. Her wonderful, inventive stories, plays and poems have delighted children of all ages for generations.

Born in London in 1897, Enid Blyton sold her first piece of literature; a poem entitled 'Have You …?' at the age of twenty. She qualified and worked as a teacher, writing extensively in her spare time. She sold short stories and poems to various magazines and her first book, *Child Whispers*, was published in 1922.

Over the next 40 years, Blyton would publish on average fifteen books a year. Some of her more famous works include *Noddy*, *The Famous Five*, *The Secret Seven* and *The Faraway Tree* series.

Her books have sold in the millions and have been translated into many languages. Enid Blyton married twice and had two daughters. She died in 1968, but her work continues to live on.

Contents

Christmas Holidays at the Farm

Four children sat looking out of a farmhouse window at the whirling snow. It was January, and a cold spell had set in. Today the snow had come, and the sky was leaden and heavy.

Rory was the biggest of the children. He was fourteen, tall and well made, and even stronger than he looked. A year's hard work on his father's farm was making him a fine youth. Then came Sheila, a year younger, who managed the hens and ducks so well that she had made quite a large sum of money out of them since the Easter before.

Benjy pressed his nose hard against the leaded panes of the old farmhouse windows. He loved the snow. 'I wonder where Scamper is,' he said.

Scamper was his pet squirrel, always to be found on his shoulder when they were together. But Scamper had been missing for a day or two.

'He's curled himself up somewhere to sleep, I expect,' said Penny, the youngest. 'Squirrels are supposed to sleep away the winter, aren't they? I'm sure you won't see him again till this cold spell has gone, Benjy.'

Penny was eight, three years younger than Benjy, so she was the baby of the family. She didn't like this at all, and was always wishing she was bigger.

'Do you think Mark will come, if it keeps snowing like this?' she asked.

Mark was a friend of theirs. He took lessons with them at the vicarage away over the fields, and the children's mother had said he might come to stay for a few days. He had never been to Willow Farm, and the children were longing to show him everything.

'Won't he be surprised to see our donkeys?' said Benjy. 'My word, mine did gallop fast this morning!'

Each of the children had a donkey, a Christmas present from their father. They had worked well on the farm, and deserved a reward—and when the four donkeys arrived on Christmas morning there had been wild excitement. The children were looking forward to riding on them when school began again. The fields had been too muddy to walk across, and they had had to go a long way round by the roads. Now they would be able to gallop there on their donkeys!

'I'm longing to show Mark over our farm,' said Rory. 'I hope this snow doesn't last too long.'

'Everywhere is beginning to look rather strange,' said Sheila. 'Snow is rather magic—it changes everything almost at once. I hope my hens are all right. I wonder what they think of the snow.'

Sheila felt sure her hens would not lay many eggs in the snowy weather. She made up her mind to give them a little extra hot mash morning and night to keep them warm. She slipped out into the kitchen to talk to Fanny about it. Fanny was the cook's niece and helped Sheila willingly with the poultry.

The snow went on falling. Soon all the farm-buildings were outlined in soft white. When their father came in to tea he shook the snow from his broad shoulders and took off his boots at the door.

'Well,' he said, 'we can't do much in this weather, except tend the beasts and see they have plenty to eat and drink. Aren't you going to help milk the cows, Benjy?'

Four children sat looking out of a farmhouse window at the whirling snow.

'Gracious, yes!' said Benjy, who was still dreaming at the window. He rushed to get his old mack and sou'-wester, and pulled on his rubber boots. Then he disappeared into the flurrying snow and made his way to the sweet-smelling cow-sheds.

Only Rory and Penny, the eldest and the youngest, were left at the window. Rory put his arm round Penny. 'Have you seen Skippetty lately?' he asked.

Skippetty was the pet lamb that Penny had had the spring and summer before. The little girl had been very fond of him, and he had followed her all over the place. But now he had grown into a sheep, and had gone to live in the fields with the others. Penny shook her head sadly.

'I don't know Skippetty when I see him!' she said. 'He's just exactly like all the others. I wish he didn't have to grow up. I miss him very much. Wasn't it fun when he used to trot at my heels everywhere?'

'Well, you'll have another pet lamb this spring, so don't worry,' said Rory. 'Won't it be lovely when the winter is over and the sun is warm again—and all the fields are green, and there are young things everywhere?'

'Yes,' said Penny happily. 'Oh, Rory, don't you love Willow Farm? Aren't you glad it's ours? Wasn't it lucky that it did so well last year?'

Her father came into the room and heard what she said. He laughed. 'Beginner's luck!' he said. 'You look out this year—maybe we shan't have such an easy time!'

4

Harriet the cook came bustling in. Fanny was out collecting the eggs with Sheila, and Harriet had come to lay the tea. She put down a dish of golden butter, and a dish of home-made cheese. Then came scones and cakes and a home-cured ham. A big jug of cream appeared, and a dish of stewed apple. Penny's eyes gleamed. This was the sort of high-tea she liked!

'Everything grown on our own farm,' she said. 'Doesn't it look good? Are you hungry, Daddy?'

'Famished!' said her father. 'Where's your mother? Ah, there she is.'

Mother had been in the icy-cold dairy and she was frozen! 'My goodness, I'm cold!' she said. 'Our dairy is wonderfully cool in the hot summer months—but I wish it was wonderfully hot in the cold winter months! I've been helping Harriet to wrap up the butter for sale. Daddy, we've done very well out of our butter-sales, you know. I feel I'd like to try my hand at something else now, as well.'

'Well, for instance?' said Daddy, pulling his chair up to the table. 'We have hens, ducks, cows, sheep, pigs, dogs and goodness knows what else! There doesn't seem much else to have.'

'Well, we haven't got bees,' said Mother, beginning to pour out the tea. 'I'd like to keep bees. I love their friendly humming—and I love their sweet yellow honey, too!'

'Oooh—bees would be fun,' said Penny. 'Oh, Mother —let's keep them this year. And we haven't got a goat. Couldn't we keep one? And what about some white pigeons? And we could have …'

'We could have a bull!' said Rory. 'Fancy, we haven't got a bull, Daddy. Aren't you going to get one?'

'One thing at a time,' said his father, cutting the ham. 'After all, we haven't had our farm a year yet. I dare say we'll have everything before the second year is out! Now, where are Sheila and Benjy?'

The two soon appeared, rosy of cheek. Benjy was pleased with his milking. He always got a wonderful froth in his pail, the sign of a good milker. He was tremendously hungry.

Sheila had good news about the hens too. 'Four more eggs today than we had yesterday,' she announced. 'Mother, the hens don't like the snow at all. They all huddle in the house together, and stare out as if they simply couldn't imagine what's happening.'

'Silly creatures, hens,' said Rory. 'Give me ducks any day! Pass the scones, Sheila.'

All the children discussed the farm-happenings with their parents. They knew all the animals and birds, they knew each field and what had been grown in each, they even knew what the sowing and manuring had cost, and what profits had been made. Each child was a keen little farmer, and not one of them was afraid of hard work. Benjy was the dreamy one, but he could work hard enough when he wanted to.

'Mark's coming tomorrow,' said Rory to his mother. 'He'd better sleep with me, hadn't he, Mother? He's never been to stay on a farm before. He lives in an ordinary house with an ordinary garden—and they don't even grow easy things like lettuces and beans. They buy everything.'

'Won't he like the things *we* grow?' said Penny. 'You know—this cheese—and that butter—and this jam—and that ham?'

'He'll like the live things better,' said Rory. 'I bet he'll like a ride on old Darling. Listen—she's coming into the yard now.'

Everyone heard the slow clip-clop of Darling's great hooves, biting through the snow on to the yard below. Everyone pictured the big, patient brown horse with her lovely brown eyes and sweeping eyelashes. They all loved Darling.

'One thing I like about farm-life,' said Benjy, cutting himself a big slab of Harriet's cream-cheese, 'is that there are so many things to love. You know, all the animals seem friends. I'd hate to live in London now, as we used to do—no great horses to rub down and talk to—no cows to milk—no lambs to watch—no hens to hear clucking—no tiny chicks and ducklings to laugh at. Golly, wouldn't I miss all our farmyard friends.'

'I wonder what Tammylan is doing in this snowy weather,' said Penny. Tammylan, the wild man, was their firm friend. He lived in a cave in the hillside, and looked after himself. All the animals of the countryside came to him, and he knew each one. The children loved visiting him, for he always had something to tell them, and something new to show them.

'We shan't be able to go and see him if the snow gets thick,' said Sheila. 'And I did want to tell him how we love our four donkeys.'

Tammylan had got the donkeys for their father to give them. He had arrived on Christmas Day, leading the

7

four fat little creatures, and had stayed for the day and then gone back to his cave.

'Won't you be lonely tonight?' Penny had asked him. But Tammylan had shaken his head.

'I've no doubt some of my animal-friends will come and sit with me this Christmas night,' he had said, and the children had pictured him sitting in his cave, lighted by a flickering candle, with perhaps a hare at his feet, a rabbit near by, and one or two birds perched up on the shelf behind his head! No animal was ever afraid of Tammylan.

Darkness came, and the children's mother lighted the big lamp. The children felt lazy and comfortable. There were no lessons to do because it was holiday-time. There was no farm-work to do because it was dark outside and snowy. They could do what they liked.

'Let's have a game of cards,' said Penny.

'No—let's read,' said Benjy.

'I'd like to sew a bit,' said Sheila.

'Well—I vote we have the radio on,' said Rory. He turned it on. There was a short silence and then a voice announced:

'This evening we are going to devote half an hour to "Work on the Farm".'

'Oh, no, we're not!' laughed Daddy, and he switched the radio off. 'This evening we're all going to play Snap! Now then—where are the cards?'

And play Snap they did, even Mother. It was good for them to forget the farm and its work for one short evening!

The Visitor

Mark arrived the next day. Rory went to meet him at the bus-stop, a mile or two away. The snow was now thick, but would soon melt, for the wind had changed. Then everywhere would be terribly muddy.

'Will you lend me Bray?' asked Rory of Benjy. 'I thought I'd ride on Neddy to meet Mark, and if you'd lend me your donkey, I could take it along for Mark to ride back on.'

'Yes, you can have him,' said Benjy. So Rory went off on Neddy, his own donkey, and Bray trotted willingly beside him. They came to the bus-stop and waited patiently for Mark. The bus came in sight after a while, and Mark jumped down carrying a small bag. He was astonished to see Rory on a grey donkey.

'Hallo, Rory,' he said. 'I didn't know you had donkeys. You never told me.'

'Well, we didn't have them till Christmas Day,' said Rory. 'Did you have a good Christmas? We did! We each got a donkey for our own. This is Neddy, the one I'm riding on. And this is Bray. He belongs to Benjy. You can ride him home.'

'Well, I've never really ridden a donkey before, except once at the seaside,' said Mark, who was smaller and fatter than Rory. 'I fell off then. Is Benjy's donkey well behaved?'

Rory laughed. 'Of course! Don't be silly, Mark! Gracious, wait till you've been on the farm a few days. You'll have ridden all the horses, and all our donkeys, too. And Buttercup the cow if you like. She doesn't mind.'

Mark had no wish to ride horses or cows. He looked doubtfully at Bray, and then tried to mount him. Bray stood quite still. Soon Mark was on his back holding tightly to the reins.

'Give me your bag,' said Rory, trying not to laugh at Mark. 'That's right. Now off we go.'

But Bray did not seem to want to move. He stood there, his ears back, flicking his tail a little. Mark yelled after Rory, who was cantering off.

'Hey! This donkey's stuck. He won't move!'

Rory cantered back. He gave Bray a push in the back with Mark's bag. 'Get up!' he said. 'You know the way home! Get up, then!'

Bray moved so suddenly that Mark nearly fell off. The donkey cantered quickly down the road, and Rory cantered after him. Soon Mark got used to the bumpity motion of the little donkey, and quite enjoyed the ride. Once he had got over his fear of falling off, he felt rather grand riding on the little donkey.

'We'll soon see the farm,' said Rory. 'It's a jolly good one. It's a mixed farm, you know.'

Mark didn't know. He wondered what a mixed farm was. 'Why is it mixed?' he said.

'Well—a mixed farm is one that keeps animals and hens and things, and grows things in the fields too,' explained Rory. 'It's the most paying sort of farm. You see, if you have a bad year with the sheep, well, you probably have a good year with the wheat. Or if you have a bad year with the potatoes, you may make it up by doing well with the poultry. We love a mixed farm, because there's always such a lot of different things to do.'

'It does sound fun,' said Mark, wishing his donkey didn't bump him quite so much. 'I shall love to see everything. I say—is that Willow Farm?'

It was. They had rounded a corner, and the farmhouse now lay before them. It was built of warm red bricks. Its thatched roof was now covered with white snow. Tall chimneys stood up from the roof. Leaded windows with green shutters were set in the walls, and Rory pointed out which belonged to his bedroom.

'You're to sleep with me,' he said. 'I've a lovely view from my room. I can see five different streams from it. All the streams have willow trees growing beside them—they are what give the farm its name.'

Mark gazed at the farmhouse and at all the old farmbuildings around—the barns and sheds, the hen-houses and other outbuildings, now white with snow. It seemed a big place to him.

'Come on,' said Rory. 'We'll put our donkeys into their shed, and go and see the others.'

Soon the five children were gathered together in Rory's bedroom, hearing Mark's news and telling him theirs. Then they took him to see the farm and all its animals.

'Come and see the horses first,' said Rory. 'I and Benjy look after them. We groom them just as well as the men could, Daddy says.'

Mark was taken to the stables and gazed rather nervously at three enormous shire-horses there.

'This is Darling, the best of the lot,' said Benjy, rubbing a big brown horse. 'And that's Captain. He's immensely strong. Stronger than any horse Daddy's ever known. And that's Blossom.'

Then Mark had to see the cows. He liked these even less than the horses because they had horns!

'See this one?' said Benjy, pointing to a soft-eyed red and white cow. 'We hope she'll have a calf this spring. We want her to have a she-calf that we can keep and rear ourselves. If she has a bull-calf we'll have to sell it. Jonquil, you'll have a little she-calf, won't you?'

'We may be going to have a big fierce bull of our own this year,' said Penny, twinkling at Mark. She guessed he wouldn't like the sound of bulls at all! He didn't. He looked round nervously as if he half expected to see a bull coming towards him, snorting fiercely!

'Well—I hope I shan't be here when the bull arrives,' he said. 'I say—what a horrid smell! What is it?'

'It's only Jim cleaning out the pig-sties,' said Sheila. 'Come and see our old sow. She had ever so many piglets in the summer—but they've all grown now. We hope she'll have some more soon. You've no idea how sweet they are!'

'*Sweet*?' said Mark in amazement. 'Surely pigs aren't sweet? I should have thought that was the last thing they were.'

'*Piglets* are sweet,' said Penny. 'They really are.'

'Well, your old sow is simply hideous,' said Mark. The five children stared at the enormous creature. The four farm children had thought she was very ugly indeed when they first saw her—but now that they were used to her and knew her so well, they thought she was nice. They felt quite cross with Mark for calling her hideous.

She grunted as she rooted round in the big sty. Mark wrinkled up his nose as he smelt the horrid smell again. 'Let's come and see something else,' he said. So they all moved off over the snowy ground to the hen-houses. Mark saw the hens sitting side by side on the perches. They did not like walking about in the snowy run.

'I manage the hens, with Fanny, our little maid,' said Sheila proudly. 'I made a lot of money through selling the eggs last year. I put some hens on ducks' eggs as well as on hens' eggs, and Fanny and I brought off heaps and heaps of chicks and ducklings.'

'Cluck-luck-luck,' said a hen.

'Yes, you did bring us luck,' said Sheila, laughing. 'Luck-luck-luck-luck!'

In the fields were big folds in which Davey the shepherd had put the sheep. He did not want them to roam too far in the snowy hills in case they got lost. Penny stood on the fence and called loudly.

'Skippetty, Skippetty, Skippetty!'

13

'She's calling the pet lamb she had last year,' explained Rory. 'Oh, Mark, do you remember when it followed her to school, like Mary's lamb in the rhyme? Wasn't that funny?'

Mark did remember. He looked to see if a little lamb was coming. But no lamb came. Instead, Davey the shepherd let a fat sheep out of the fold. It came trotting across the snowy grass to Penny.

'Penny! This isn't your lamb, is it?' cried Mark, in surprise. 'Gracious! It's a big heavy sheep now.'

'I know,' said Penny regretfully. 'When I remember that dear little frisky, long-leggitty creature that drank out of a baby's milk-bottle, I can hardly believe this sheep was once that lamb. I think it's very sad.'

'Yes, it is,' said Mark. Skippetty put his nose through the fence and nuzzled against Penny's legs. To him Penny was still the dear little girl who had been his companion all through the spring and summer before. She hadn't changed as he had.

'I wish I could show you my tame squirrel,' said Benjy. 'He's been missing the last few days. We think he may be sleeping the cold spell away.'

'Oh, I've seen Scamper, you know,' said Mark, remembering the times when Benjy had brought him to school on his shoulder. 'Whistle to him as you used to do. Maybe he'll come. Even if he's asleep some-where surely he will hear your whistle and wake!'

'Well, I've whistled lots of times,' said Benjy. 'But I'll whistle again if you like.'

14

The Visitor

So the boy stood in the farmyard and whistled. He had a very special whistle for Scamper the squirrel, low and piercing, and very musical. Tammylan the wild man had taught him the whistle. The five children stood still and waited.

Benjy whistled again—and then, over the snow, his tail spread out behind him, scampered the tame squirrel. He had been sleeping in a hole in a near-by willow tree—but not very soundly. Squirrels rarely sleep all the winter through. They wake up at intervals to find their hidden stores of food, and have a feed. Scamper had heard Benjy's whistle in his dreams, and had awakened.

Then down the tree he came with a flying leap, and made his way to the farmyard, bounding along as light as a feather.

'Oh, here he is!' yelled Benjy in delight. The squirrel sprang to his shoulder with a little chattering noise and nibbled the bottom of Benjy's right ear. He adored the boy. Mark gazed at him in envy. How he wished he had a pet wild creature who would go to him like that. 'Would he come to me?' he asked.

'Yes,' said Benjy, and patted Mark's shoulder. The squirrel leapt to it, brushed against Mark's hair, and sprang back to Benjy's shoulder again.

'Lovely!' said Mark. 'I wish he was mine.'

A bell rang down at the farmhouse. 'That's Harriet ringing to tell us dinner's ready,' said Rory. 'Come on. I'm jolly hungry.'

15

'So am I,' said Mark. 'I could eat as much as that old sow there!'

'Well, I hope you won't make such a noise when you're eating as *she* does!' said Benjy. 'Listen to her! We've never been able to teach her table-manners—have we, Penny?'

An Exciting Time

It was thrilling for Mark to wake up in Rory's bedroom the next morning and hear all the farmyard sounds, though they were somewhat muffled by the snow. He heard the sound of the horses, the far-off mooing of the cows, and the clucking of the hens. The ducks quacked sadly because their pond was frozen.

'I wish I lived on a farm always,' thought Mark. He looked across to Rory's bed. The boy was awake and sat up. He looked at his watch. 'Time to get up,' he said.

'What, so early!' said Mark, in dismay. 'It's quite dark.'

'Ah, you have to be up and about early on a farm,' said Rory, leaping out of bed. 'Jim and Bill have been up ages already—and as for Davey the shepherd, I guess he's been awake for hours!'

Mark dressed with Rory and they went down to join the others, who were already at the breakfast-table. Rory's father had had his breakfast and gone out. The children sat and ate and chattered.

'What would Mark like to do today?' said Sheila politely, looking at Rory. 'It's too cold for a picnic. One day we'll take him to see Tammylan, the wild man. But not today.'

'Oh, I don't want you to plan anything special for me at all,' said Mark hastily. 'I don't want to be treated as a visitor. Just let me do things you all do. That would be much more fun for me.'

'All right,' said Rory. 'I dare say you are right. I remember when we all went from London to stay for a while at our uncle's farm, the year before last, we simply loved doing the ordinary little things—feeding the hens and things like that. You shall do just the same as we do. Sheila, you take him with you after breakfast.'

'He can help me to scrape all the perches,' said Sheila. 'And he can wash the eggs too.'

'I want to do that,' said Penny. 'Since the calves that I looked after have grown up, there isn't much for me to do.'

'Davey the shepherd will let you have another lamb soon,' said Mother. 'Then you can hand-feed it and look after it as you looked after Skippetty last year. You will soon be busy.'

'And you can come and milk a cow this afternoon, Mark,' promised Benjy. 'We'll see if you are a good milker or not.'

Mark wasn't sure he wanted to milk a cow. He thought all animals with horns looked dangerous. But he didn't like to seem a coward, so he nodded his head.

'Have you finished your breakfast?' asked Sheila. 'Have another bit of toast? You've only had four. We've all had about six.'

'No, thanks,' said Mark, whose appetite was not quite so enormous as that of the other children. 'Are you going to do the hens now, Sheila? Shall I get ready?'

The children sat and ate and chattered.

'Have you brought some old things?' asked Sheila. 'Good. Well, put on an old coat and your rubber boots and a scarf. I'll go and get ready too.'

It wasn't long before both children were on their way to the hen-house, each carrying a pailful of hot mash that Harriet the cook had given them. The snow was now melting and the yard was in a fearful state of slush. The children slithered about in it.

'Oh, isn't this awful?' said Sheila. 'Snow is lovely when it's white and clean—but when it goes into slush it's simply horrid. Mark—be careful, you silly!'

At Sheila's shout, Mark looked where he was going. He had turned his head to watch Jim the farm-hand, taking a cart full of mangels out of the yard—and he walked straight into an enormous, slushy puddle near the pig-sty. He tried to leap aside, and the pail of mash caught his legs and sent him over. In a trice he was in the puddle, and the pail of mash emptied itself over his legs.

'Mark! What a mess you're in!' cried Sheila in dismay. Mark scrambled up and looked down at himself. His coat was soaked with horrid-smelling dampness, and his rubber boots were full of hot hen-mash. He was almost ready to cry!

'Don't worry,' said Sheila. 'Your coat will dry.'

'I'm not bothered about that,' said Mark. 'I'm bothered about the waste of that hot mash. Just look at it, all over the place.'

'You go in and ask Mother to lend you some old clothes of Rory's,' said Sheila comfortingly. 'I'll get a spade out of the shed and just get most of the spilt mash

20

back into the pail. It will be dirty, but I don't expect the hens will mind very much.'

Mark disappeared into the house. Sheila shovelled up most of the spilt mash. She took it to the hen-houses and the hens came down from their houses into the slushy rain, clucking hungrily.

'I'll let you out into the farmyard to scratch about there as you usually do,' said Sheila, who had always talked to her hens as if they were children. 'Your yard is nothing but mud—but so is everywhere else. Now then, greedy—take your head out of the bucket!'

Sheila put the mash into the big bowls, and then broke the ice on the water-bowls. There had been a frost in the night, and the ice had not yet melted. She went to get a can to put in fresh water. The hens clucked round it.

'I know that your water must always be clean and fresh,' said Sheila to her hens. 'Look—there's the cock calling to you. He's found something for you!'

The cock was a beautiful bird, with an enormous, drooping tail of purple-green feathers, and a fine comb. He had a very loud voice, and always awoke all his hens in the morning when it was time to get up. Now he had found a grain of corn or some other titbit on the ground and he was telling the hens to come and eat it.

Mark arrived again, wearing an old brown coat of Rory's, and somebody else's boots. 'Look at the cock,' said Sheila. 'He's a perfect gentleman, Mark—he never eats a titbit himself—he always calls his hens to have it.'

'Cock-a-doodle-doo!' said the cock to Mark.

'He's saying "Good morning, how do you do?" said Sheila, with a laugh. She always amused the others because whenever her hens or ducks clucked or quacked, she always made it seem as if they were really saying something. Penny honestly thought that they said the things Sheila made up, and she felt that they were really very clever.

'Come and scrape the perches for me,' said Sheila. 'The hens haven't very good manners, you know, and they make their perches in an awful mess.'

Mark had the job of scraping the perches clean. He wasn't sure that he liked it much, but he was a sensible boy and knew that there were dirty jobs to do as well as nice ones. You can't pick your jobs on a farm. You have to be ready to do everything!

Sheila looked to see if there was enough grit in the little box she kept for that purpose. She told Mark what it was for. 'It's to help the hens digest their food properly,' she told him. 'And that broken oyster-shell over there is to help them to make good shells for their eggs. Take this basket of eggs indoors into the kitchen, Mark. You can begin to wash them for me. Some of them are awfully dirty.'

Poor Mark broke one of the eggs as he washed it! It just slipped out of his fingers. He was upset about it, but Sheila said, 'Never mind! We brought in twenty-three eggs, and that's very good for a day like this.'

Mark soon began to enjoy the life on the farm very much. The days slipped by, and he was sad when Saturday came and he packed to go home. Then, quite unexpectedly, his mother telephoned to ask if he could be kept there a little longer as his grandmother was ill, and she wanted to go and look after her.

'Oh,' said Mark in delight, 'oh, do you think I *can* stay? If I can, I promise I'll do my best to help on the farm. I'll even clean out the pig-sties!'

Everyone laughed at that, for they knew how Mark hated the smell. 'Of course you can stay,' said Mother, who liked the quiet but rather awkward little boy. 'You are really quite useful, especially since you have learnt how to milk.'

It was a very funny thing, but Mark had been most successful at milking the cows. He had been terrified at first, and had gone quite pale when he had sat down on a milking-stool, and had watched whilst Benjy showed him how to squeeze the big teats and make the milk squirt down into the great clean pails.

He couldn't get a drop of milk at first—and then suddenly it had come, and Mark had jumped when he heard the milk go splash-splash into the pail. The boy's hands were strong, and he just seemed to have the right knack for milking. Jim the farm-hand had praised him, and Mark had felt proud.

'Milking is quite hard work,' he said to Penny. And what a lot you get! Isn't it creamy too? No wonder you are able to make a lot of butter.'

All the children worked during the holidays, and they disliked the slush and wet very much. Rain had come after the snow, and everywhere was squelchy, so that it was no pleasure to go round the farm and do anything.

The farm-hands were splashed with mud from head to foot, and the old shire-horses had to be cleaned well every day, for they too were covered with mud.

'I shall be quite glad when it's time to go to school again,' said Rory, coming in one day with his coat soaked, and his hair dripping. 'Farming really isn't much fun in this weather. I've been cleaning out our donkey-stable. Mark's been helping me. He kept holding his nose till he found the smell wasn't bad after all. Daddy says the manure will be marvellous for the kitchen-garden, where Mother grows her lettuces and things.'

'Nothing's wasted on a farm, is it?' said Mark. 'Jim told me yesterday that he takes all the wood-ash for that field called Long Bottom. He says it's just what the soil wants there. And Bill is piling the soot from the chimneys into sacks in that shed behind the donkeys. He says you will use that somewhere on the farm too.'

Mark was learning a great deal, and liked airing what he had learnt. He had ridden all the donkeys now, and all the horses too—though that wasn't very difficult, for the shire-horses had backs like sofas! He wouldn't ride on Buttercup the cow. The children themselves were not supposed to, but actually Buttercup didn't mind at all. She was a placid old lady, and loved having children round her.

The Christmas holidays only had a day or two more to go. The children began to get out their pencil-boxes and pile together their books. All of them went to the vicarage for lessons, but later on, perhaps in the autumn, the two boys were going to boarding-school again. They hated to think of this, and never talked about it.

Mark was to go home after the first day at school. The others were sorry, for it had been fun to show him all round Willow Farm. Mark was sad too. He knew all the animals there by now, and it was such a nice friendly feeling to go out and talk to a horse or a cow, or to Rascal, the shepherd's clever dog.

'If only holidays lasted for always!' he sighed. But alas, they never do!

The New Horses

'You know, I *must* get a couple of strong horses for light work,' said the farmer, one morning at breakfast, as the children were hurrying to get off to school. Rory had gone out to get the donkeys, so he was not there. 'It's silly to use our big shire-horses for light cart-work. We really could do with a couple of smaller horses.'

'Oooh, how lovely!' said Penny, who always welcomed any addition to the farm's livestock. 'Oh, Daddy, do let me go with you.'

'I shall go on Wednesday afternoon,' said her father. 'It's market-day then. You'll be at school, little Penny.'

'I shan't, I shan't!' squeaked Penny. 'It's a half-holiday this week. I shall come with you. I do love market-day. Will you use one of the new horses for the milk-round, Daddy?'

'Yes, I shall,' said her father. The children were all very interested in the sale of their milk. Some of it was cooled, and put into big churns to be sent away to the large towns—and some of it was delivered to people near by who were willing to buy the good creamy milk of the farm.

Sometimes their father grumbled and sighed because he had so many papers to fill in about his cows and their milk. He had inspectors to examine his cow-sheds, and other men to examine and test his cows to make sure they were healthy.

'You see,' he explained to the children, 'I want my milk to be as perfect as it can be, free from any bad germs that might make people ill. Well, you can only get milk like that if you buy the right cows who come from good stock, and are healthy and strong, and good milkers. Our cows are fine, but our cow-sheds could be made much better.'

'How could they, Daddy?' asked Benjy, in surprise. He always liked the old, rather dark cow-sheds. They smelt of cow, and it was cosy in there, milking on a winter's day, whilst the cows munched away happily.

'I'd like to take them down and put up clean, airy sheds,' said his father. 'I'd like cow-sheds where you could eat your dinner off the floor, it would be so clean! Well—maybe if I get a good price for the potatoes I've got stored, I can think about the cow-sheds. And you can help me then, Benjy and Rory! We'll think out some lovely sheds, and get books to see what kind are the best.'

'Oooh yes,' said Benjy. 'We'd have more cows then, wouldn't we, Daddy? Sixteen isn't very many, really, though it seemed a lot at first. Daddy, I wish you'd let me and Rory do the milk-round on Saturdays once or twice. It would be such fun.'

'Oh no—Jim has time enough for that,' said his father. 'But if he's ever too busy, as he may be when the spring comes again, I'll let you try. You had better go with him once or twice to see what he does.'

'Can we all go to the market with you to buy our new horses?' asked Sheila eagerly.

'Yes, if you like,' said their father. 'I shall go in the car. You can go on your donkeys. Look—there they are at the door, waiting for you.'

'Sheila! Benjy! Penny!' shouted Rory impatiently. 'Aren't you ever coming? We shall be late.'

The children tore out to their donkeys. 'Hallo, Canter!' said Sheila, giving him a lump of sugar. 'Did you sleep well?'

'Frrrrumph!' said the donkey, nuzzling against Sheila's shoulder.

'He said yes, he had an awfully good night,' said Sheila to the others.

Penny turned to her donkey too. 'Did you sleep well, darling Hee-Haw?' she asked.

'Frrrrrumph!' said her donkey too, and tried to nibble at her sleeve.

'Oh, Hee-Haw didn't have at all a good night,' said Penny solemnly, turning to the others. 'He says a mouse ran over his back all night long.'

The others laughed. 'Now don't *you* begin making up things like Sheila!' said Rory. 'Do come on, Sheila. What's the matter? Is your saddle loose?'

'A bit,' said Sheila, tightening it. 'Rory, Daddy's going to the market on Wednesday to buy two new light horses—not cart-horses—and we can go with him!'

'Good!' said Rory, galloping off in front. 'I love the market. Get up, Neddy, get up—you're not as fast as you usually are, this morning!'

The New Horses

The children were glad when they galloped home after morning school on Wednesday. A half-holiday was always nice—but going to the market made it even nicer. They ate a hurried lunch, and then went out to get their donkeys again. Their father set off in his car and told them where to meet him.

The donkeys were ready for a run, and a run they had, for it was quite a long way to the town where the market was held. The little fat grey creatures were glad to be tethered to a post when the children arrived at the market. Rory went round them to make sure they were safely tethered, for it would not be easy to trace a lost donkey in a big crowded market.

They soon found their father, who was talking to a man about the horses he needed. He went to the part of the market where patient horses were standing ready for sale. The boys went with him and the girls went to look at some fat geese cackling near by. There were no geese at Willow Farm, and Sheila longed to have some to add to her hens and ducks.

'They only eat things like grass, you know,' said Sheila. 'They are awfully cheap to keep.'

'They're very hissy, aren't they?' said Penny, who wasn't quite sure about the big birds.

'You are a baby, Penny!' laughed Sheila. 'You always say that when you see geese. Why shouldn't they hiss and cackle? It's their way of talking.'

'What are they saying?' asked Penny, looking at the big birds.

'They're saying, "Ss-ss-sss-it's funny Penny's frightened of us-ss-ss-sss!" ' said Sheila solemnly.

Meanwhile the boys were looking at horses with their father and his farmer friend. Horses of all colours and sizes were paraded up and down in front of them. Benjy liked a little brown one with gentle eyes. She had good legs and he was sure she was just the right horse for the milk-round.

'She'd be good for the milk-round, Daddy,' he said. 'I'm sure she'd soon learn what houses to stop at without being told!'

'Oh, it's for a milk-round you want her, is it?' said the man.

'Among other things,' answered the farmer.

'You can't do better than have that little brown horse then,' said the man. 'She's been used to a milk-round already. She's strong and healthy, and as gentle as a lamb.'

So little Ebony was chosen, and Benjy was delighted. He mounted her at once and she put her head round and looked at him inquiringly out of her large brown eyes, as if to say, 'Hallo! I'm yours now, am I?'

The other horse chosen was an ugly fellow, but healthy and good-tempered. He was brown and white in patches, and had long legs and bony hindquarters. He moved in an ungainly manner, but it was plain that he had great strength.

'He's a good stayer,' said the man who owned him. 'He'll work till he drops. He's done more work on my farm than any other horse, and that's saying something. I wish I hadn't had to let him go—but I need cart-horses, not light horses.'

The New Horses

So Patchy was bought too, at a fair price, and the man promised to take them both back to the farm that evening. Rory paused to look at a magnificently-built horse in a near-by stall. The horse looked at him and then rolled his eyes so that the whites showed.

'Daddy, this is the finest-looking horse in the market,' said Rory. 'I wonder why he isn't sold!'

'He's bad-tempered,' said his father. 'Look how he rolls his eyes at you. Keep out of the way of his hind-feet! Nobody wants a bad-tempered horse, because so often he is stupid, though he may be strong and healthy. I'd rather work a horse like Patchy, ugly though he is, than this magnificent creature.'

The children wandered round the market before they went back to their donkeys. It was such an exciting place, and so noisy at times that they had to shout to one another to make themselves heard!

Sheep baaed loudly and continuously. Cows mooed and bellowed. A great strong bull, safely roped to his stall, stamped impatiently. The children watched him from a safe distance.

'I do wish we had a bull,' said Rory. 'I'm sure a farm isn't a proper farm without a bull.'

'I'll get one in the spring,' said his father. 'He can live in the orchard. My word, look at those beautiful goats!'

In a pen by themselves were three beautiful milk-white goats. Penny immediately longed for one.

'I don't think a farm is a farm unless it has goats, too,' she announced. 'Daddy, do buy me a goat when I have a birthday.'

'I'll buy you a baby-goat, a kid, when it's your birthday,' said her father. 'Yes, I promise I will. Now, don't go quite mad, Penny—you may be sorry you've got a goat when it grows up. They can be a great nuisance.'

Penny flung her arms round her father's waist and hugged him. The thought of the kid filled her with joy for the rest of the day. She tried to think out all kinds of names for it, and the others became impatient when she recited them.

'Penny, do wait till you get the kid,' said Sheila. 'What is the good of thinking of a name like Blackie when the kid may be as white as snow? Don't be silly.'

When they had seen everything in the market and had looked at the big sows there and wondered if their own sow at home was as big, the children made their way back to their donkeys.

'Well, it's been a lovely afternoon,' said Penny. 'Goodness, it's cold now. Gee-up, Hee-Haw. Gallop along and bump me and get me warm!'

Whilst the children were sitting eating their high-tea, there came the noise of hooves, and a knock at the back-door.

'The new horses!' squealed Penny and rushed out to see. 'I'm going to give them each a carrot to let them know they've come to a nice farm. Harriet, can I take two carrots? Oh, thank you. Here you are, Patchy; here you are, Ebony. Crunch them up. Welcome to Willow Farm!'

'Well, Missy, if that's the sort of welcome you give horses, they'll work well for you!' said the man who had brought them. Jim appeared at that moment and took the horses off to their stable. They both looked round at Penny as they went, and said, 'Hrrrrumph!'

'They told me they were very pleased to come here!' Penny told the others. 'They really did!'

Darling in Trouble

The two new horses settled down well. They put their noses to the muzzles of the big plough horses and seemed to talk to one another.

'I suppose that's their way of shaking hands,' said Penny, watching them. 'I do like the way animals nose one another. I wish we could do that too.'

'Our noses aren't big enough,' said Benjy. 'Besides, we'd always be catching colds from one another if we did that.'

'Animals don't,' said Penny. 'I don't think I've ever seen an animal with a cold now I come to think of it.'

'Well, I have,' said Benjy. 'I've seen dogs and cats with colds—and I've seen Rascal when he had a tummy-ache too.'

'It's a good thing horses don't get the tummy-ache,' said Penny. 'They've such big tummies, haven't they?'

Her father overheard what she said and laughed. 'Oh, horses do get ill,' he said. 'It's tiresome when they do, though—they're such big creatures, and kick about so. Thank goodness none of mine have ever been ill.'

It was a funny thing that the farmer said that, because that very night Darling, the biggest horse, was taken ill in her stable.

Darling in Trouble

It was Benjy who found out that Darling was ill. He had rubbed her down with Rory, when the three plough horses came in from the field, and had watched them eat their meal.

'Isn't Darling hungry?' he said to Rory. 'She always gobbles, but tonight she is eating twice as fast as the others. Darling, don't gobble!'

Darling twitched back a big brown ear, but went on gobbling. She really was very hungry indeed, for she had been working hard in the wet fields all day. The boys gave each horse a slap behind and a kind word and went out. They had rubbed down the two new horses too. Patchy and Ebony liked the children very much, especially little Penny, who was always talking to them and bringing them titbits.

As usual the family went to bed early, even the grown-ups being in bed and asleep by ten o'clock. Nobody heard the noise from the stables—except Benjy. He suddenly awoke, hearing some unusual sound.

He lay for a little while in his small bedroom, wondering what had awakened him. Then the sound came again—a sound he had never in his life heard before! He couldn't imagine what it was like.

'What *is* it?' thought the boy, sitting up in alarm. 'It's somebody—or something—groaning—but who can it be? It's such a funny deep groan.'

Then he heard another noise—the sound of hooves against wood, and he leapt out of bed.

'I must see what it is,' he thought. He put on a thick coat, took his torch, found his shoes, and slipped out

35

down the stairs. He undid the big front door and ran into the wet yard. The noise of groans was now much more clearly heard. The boy ran to the stables and opened the door. He switched on his torch, and saw a sight that shocked him.

The great plough horse, Darling, was lying on the floor of the stable, groaning terribly, and gasping as if for breath. She moved her hooves as she groaned and these struck the wooden partition between her stall and the next. The other horses were standing quietly in their own stalls, puzzled by the sounds that came from Darling.

'Oh, Darling, whatever's the matter?' cried Benjy. The big horse took no notice of the boy, but lay with her hooves twitching curiously. Benjy sensed at once that the horse was really ill. He tore out of the stable and went to wake his father.

In two minutes the farmer was in the stable, bending over Darling. 'She's got colic,' he said.

'What's colic?' asked Benjy.

'Just what I said my horses had never had!' said the farmer, with a groan. 'Tummy-ache! And Penny was right when she said it must be dreadful for horses to have that. It is! Very dreadful.'

'Will Darling die?' asked Benjy, in a whisper. It really seemed to him as if the horse was dying under his eyes.

'She will if we don't save her,' said his father. 'Go and get Jim and Bill. Quick now. We've got to get Darling on her feet. She'll die if she lies there. We've got to get her up. I can't do it by myself.'

'Oh Darling, whatever's the matter?' cried Benjy.

Very frightened, Benjy sped to the cottages where the two farm-hands lived. It wasn't long before they were in the stable with the farmer.

'We must get Darling on to her feet,' said the farmer. 'Come on, Jim, you get to her head. Bill, slap her on the rump—hard. Go on, hard! I'll help Jim. Come on now, old girl—up you get!'

But Darling didn't get up. Instead she began to groan and pant again, and the awful noises made poor Benjy feel quite sick. The three men heaved and hauled, and the great horse made no attempt to help them at all. She felt too ill to stand and she just wasn't *going* to stand. The men gave up after a while and stood exhausted by the horse, panting almost as loudly as the great animal.

'Go and telephone the vet, Benjy,' said his father, wiping the perspiration off his forehead. 'Tell him Darling has colic and ask him to come as quickly as possible. Good heavens, this horse is worth a lot of money—we can't afford to lose her!'

'Oh, Daddy, who cares about the money!' cried Benjy, almost in tears. 'If she was only worth a little, we'd have to save her because we love her!'

'Of course, silly boy,' said his father. 'Now go quickly and tell the vet to come. Jim—Bill—let's try again to get Darling up.'

'She's that heavy and obstinate,' grunted Jim. He was a tiny fellow, with immensely broad shoulders and long strong arms. He began to try and get Darling up, helped by the others. The horse seemed to realise what the men were doing this time, and herself tried to rise. She fell back again with a thud and put her great patient head to the ground, groaning deeply.

'Poor creature,' said Bill. 'She's in a bad way, sure enough.'

'I hope the vet comes quickly,' said the farmer, leaning exhausted against the stall. 'Ah—here's Benjy back again. What did the vet say, lad?'

'Oh, Daddy, he's out to a farm twenty miles the other way,' said Benjy, his eyes full of tears. 'So I rang up the other man who came here once—but he's ill in bed and can't possibly come. He said we were to keep the horse on her feet and walk her up and down, up and down till we got someone to come and give her what he called a "drench".'

'Get her on her feet!' growled Jim, looking at the poor horse lying flat down, her hooves twitching. 'That's easier said than done. Come on—we must try again. She's getting worse.'

Bill had an idea that pulling her up with ropes would be a good plan, so the three men between them tried that next—and with a terrifying groan Darling was at last got to her feet. She stood there, swaying as if she was going to fall down the next moment.

'Get her out of the stable and walk her round a bit,' gasped the farmer. 'We mustn't let her get down again. Open the door wide, Benjy.'

Benjy opened it, and the great plough horse staggered out, swaying, her head hanging down in a pathetic manner.

'Daddy, what's made her like this?' asked Benjy. 'It's awful.'

'She eats too fast,' said his father. 'It doesn't sound anything much, I know, to say she has eaten too fast— but a horse can die of the colic brought on by that. And Darling's pretty bad. Hold up there, my pretty—hold up. Jim, go the other side. She's swaying over.'

It was a terrible business to keep the great horse on her feet. Whenever it seemed as if Darling was going to fall over again, or appeared to want to lie down because she really wasn't going to stand or walk about any more, the farmer shouted loud words of command at her, and the well-trained horse tried to obey them. Jim and Bill slapped her smartly too, and the poor old horse somehow managed to keep on her feet and stagger round the farmyard, making a great noise with her feet. The sounds awoke everyone in the house, and one by one, Harriet, Fanny, Mother, and the other children came out to see whatever was the matter.

'Go back to bed,' ordered the farmer. 'You can none of you do anything. You go too, Benjy.'

'I can't, Daddy, I can't,' said Benjy. 'I love Darling so much. I can't go back to bed till I know she won't die. I can't.'

'When is that vet coming?' said Jim, who by now was getting very tired. 'You left a message for him, didn't you, Benjy?'

'Of course,' said Benjy. 'But goodness knows when he'd be back and get my message.'

'Horse'll be dead by that time!' said Bill gloomily. 'Whoa there, my lady. Oh—down she goes again!'

40

With a terrific thud the horse half fell and half lay down. She lay there in the mud of the yard, her hooves kicking feebly by the light of the big lantern.

'And now we've got to get her up again,' groaned the farmer. 'Benjy, is that you still there? I told you to go to bed. Go on now—you can't do anything to help, and it's only making you miserable to watch us.'

'Please, Daddy,' began Benjy. But his father cut him short angrily, for he was tired and worried.

'Do as you're told—and at once!'

Benjy fled away into the darkness, very unhappy. He went up to his bedroom, thinking of the great horse that he and Rory loved to brush and comb each day. He remembered her soft brown eyes and long eyelashes. She was the dearest horse in the world—and she might not get better if the vet didn't come quickly and cure her.

No sooner had Benjy got into bed, as cold as ice, than a thought came to him that made him sit up and shiver with excitement. Why, oh why hadn't he thought of it before? He would go and fetch Tammylan, the wild man. Tammylan knew how to handle all animals—he knew how to cure them—he knew everything about them. Tammylan, oh, Tammylan, you must come and help old Darling.

Benjy put on a coat again, and his rubber boots. He wound a scarf round his head and neck, for the night really was very cold. He took his torch and slipped down the stairs for the second time that night. Then out into the yard and away up the lane as fast as he could!

'I hope I don't lose the way in the dark,' thought the boy desperately. 'Everything looks so different when it's night-time.'

Tammylan's cave was about two miles away. Benjy ran panting up to the top of Willow Hill, and then across Christmas Common, which looked strange in the starlight. If only Tammylan was in his cave! If only he would come! Then Darling would be saved and wouldn't die. Oh, Tammylan, do be in your cave, do be in your cave!

Tammylan Comes

It was difficult to find exactly where the wild man's cave was at night. It was always well hidden in the hillside, for Tammylan did not like his dwelling-place to be easily seen. He liked to live alone in peace and happiness with his friends, the wild animals and birds. Benjy flashed his torch over the dead heather and lank grass growing on the hillside, trying to find the entrance to the cave.

'There it is!' said the boy thankfully, at last, and he made his way to it, calling as he went. 'Tammylan! Oh, Tammylan! Are you there?'

There was no answer. Tammylan must be asleep. Benjy didn't dare to think he might not be there. He stumbled into the dark cave and flashed his torch around. There was the wild man's rough couch of dead bracken and heather, with a knitted blanket thrown over it. Sheila and Penny had made that for him. And there was the little carved stool that the two boys had made for him—and Tammylan's small collection of dishes and tin plates.

But no Tammylan. The couch was empty. The cave had nobody there except a small mouse who sat up and looked at Benjy with brown eyes.

'If only you could tell me where Tammylan is!' said Benjy desperately to the mouse. 'What bad luck to find him away just this one night!'

He went out of the cave and stood in the starlight. He called loudly and despairingly.

'Tammylan! Tammy-lan!'

He listened, but there was no answer anywhere. 'This is like a bad dream,' thought the boy. 'A dream where something horrid happens, and everything goes wrong, and you can't put it right, no matter what you do. I wonder if I *am* dreaming!'

But he wasn't. The stars twinkled down. An owl called somewhere. Sheep baaed on the hillside far away. Benjy felt very much alone and very sad.

'I must go home,' he thought. 'I can't stay here all night waiting for the wild man. I'll just give one long whistle first—the way he taught me—and then go.'

He pursed up his lips, took in a deep breath, and gave the piercing, musical whistle that Tammylan had taught him, the same whistle he used when he wanted to call Scamper, his squirrel. And oh, how wonderful—an answering whistle came back through the night— Tammylan's whistle!

Benjy almost wept for joy. He whistled again, trying to put as much urgency into it as possible, and once more the answering call came back, fluting through the starlit night.

Then Benjy had a shock. Something ran up his body and jumped to his shoulder, chattering softly. For a moment the boy stiffened in fright—and then he cried out in joy and relief. 'Scamper! Where were you? You've been missing again, and now you've come back. You heard my whistle, didn't you—but I was really whistling for Tammylan, not for you. And Tammylan's coming! He's coming!'

The squirrel chattered softly against Benjy's ear and his warmth was very comforting to the boy.

He suddenly felt happy and called loudly, 'Tammylan! Is it you?'

And a voice answered from a distance. 'I'm coming, Benjy, I'm coming!' In two minutes the wild man was standing beside the boy, his arm round his shoulders, questioning him anxiously.

'What's the matter? Why have you come to me at this hour of the night?'

'Oh, Tammylan, it's poor Darling,' said Benjy, and he poured out the whole story. Tammylan listened without a word to the end.

'If the vet doesn't come till the morning Darling will certainly die,' he said. 'I'll come with you and bring her some medicine of my own making.'

'The vet said she wanted a "drench", Tammylan,' said Benjy. 'What did he mean? Did he mean a bath?'

'No—medicine to put her tummy right,' said Tammylan, and he disappeared into his cave. 'I've got what she needs—not quite what the vet would give her, perhaps—but it will set her right in no time!'

He took down a tin, whose lid was very tightly screwed on. He opened it and took down another tin. He shook some powder from one tin into the other, and then swiftly made up some concoction that smelt rather strong. 'Now come along,' he said to Benjy. 'Every minute may count. Hurry!'

They hurried. It was much easier to go with Tammylan than to go alone. It seemed hardly any time before the lights of Willow Farm showed below them, as they went over the top of Willow Hill.

'I can see the light of the big lantern in the yard,' panted Benjy. 'That means that Darling is still there. I wonder if they got her on her feet again. Oh, Tammylan—I hope we're not too late.'

'I can hear her groaning,' said Tammylan, who had ears as sharp as a hare's. They hurried down to the farm and went into the yard where the three men were still struggling to keep Darling walking about. They had managed to get her on her feet once more.

'Who's that?' called the farmer sharply, as he saw the two figures by the light of the lantern. 'Is it the vet?'

'No. It's Tammylan,' said the wild man, and he stepped up to the gasping, groaning horse. 'She's bad, isn't she? I've got something to give her. You can't wait till the vet comes. You must trust me to give her what she needs.'

Bill and Jim looked at Tammylan rather suspiciously. But the farmer knew him well and heaved a sigh of relief. 'Well, I don't know that you'll be able to do anything, Tammylan—she's pretty well exhausted now.'

The horse was so enormous that the wild man could not give her the 'drench' from where he stood on the ground. The men had to lead the horse to a near-by cart and Tammylan mounted the wagon and waited for the horse's head to be swung round to him.

Darling did not want anything more done to her—but Tammylan's voice reached her half-fainting mind. She pricked her ears feebly and turned towards the wild man. All animals heeded his voice, wild or tame. In a trice Tammylan had given her the medicine, helped by Jim, Bill, and the farmer, who held on valiantly to the struggling horse. She swallowed with a great deal of noise, and jerked her head hard.

'Now keep her walking,' said Tammylan. 'Here—let me take her for a while. You must all be tired out. I'll see she doesn't lie down again.'

Harriet came out with a can of hot tea. The three tired men turned to her eagerly. Tammylan took the horse by the bridle and firmly walked her round the yard, talking to her in his low voice.

'Could I have some tea too, Daddy?' said a small voice, and Benjy came out of the shadows.

'So *you* fetched Tammylan, did you?' said his father, pouring out some tea for the small boy. 'Well, it was a good idea—a very good idea indeed. Here you are—drink this up. My word, it took three of us to keep that horse on her feet this last hour or two—and there's Tammylan handling her all by himself. He's a marvel, no doubt about that.'

Benjy sat contentedly by his father, sipping his hot tea. He listened to the men talking and felt very grown-up. To be out here in the yard, long past midnight, having tea with three men was marvellous—and he felt

47

happy now that Tammylan was there. Tammylan could put things right—he could put things—

Benjy's head fell forward and he was asleep. He was awakened by a laugh. Then he heard a curious sound. 'It's rather like the band tuning up before it plays,' thought the boy drowsily. 'I wonder if the band is going to play.' Then he sat up straight, wide awake. 'But there isn't a band, of course. How silly I am. Well, what's that noise then?'

He said these last words out loud and his father laughed again.

'The medicine is working inside old Darling,' he said.

'That's her innards making music,' said Jim, with a chuckle. 'She'll be all right now, so she will.'

It was simply amazing to hear the strange musical noises that came from inside the enormous horse as Tammylan walked her firmly round the yard. Darling groaned once or twice more, but not so deeply as before.

'She'll be all right now,' said the farmer. 'And this time you really *must* go to bed, Benjy. That's definite. If you don't, I'll give you some of the medicine that Tammylan's brought for Darling!'

Benjy stood up, laughing. He felt very contented and happy. Darling was safe. She wouldn't die. He had saved her by getting Tammylan. He ran across to the wild man and put his hand in his. Scamper was on Tammylan's shoulder, and leapt to Benjy with a little cry of delight.

'I'm going to bed,' he said. 'Oh, Tammylan, I'm so glad you came. Thank you ever so much.'

'I'm glad I could help,' said the wild man, still firmly walking Darling about, whilst strange noises gurgled and sang inside her. 'You go off now, Benjy—and don't you dare to get up early tomorrow morning. You can't have had any sleep tonight.'

Benjy went back to bed again. He was so tired that he didn't think of taking off his old coat and scarf, though he managed to remove his boots. He fell asleep half dressed, intending to be down bright and early for breakfast, to tell all the others what had happened in the night.

But he didn't awake in time—and nobody dreamt of waking the tired boy. Mother told Harriet to keep his breakfast hot till he awoke.

Benjy didn't wake up until ten o'clock! It was the clock downstairs striking that awoke him. He stretched himself lazily and rubbed his eyes. The early sunshine came into his room, lighting up everything, and he sat up, puzzled.

Usually it was dark, these winter mornings, when he woke up. How was it that the sun was in the room? He looked at his watch. Golly! Ten o'clock! Then, in a flood, he remembered the happenings of the night before, threw off the old coat, and was out of bed in a twink, and downstairs, in his pyjamas.

'Mother! Mother! Where are you? Is Darling all right? Mother! Where are you?'

And then he caught sight of something that pleased and relieved him enormously. It was Darling herself, looking rather sad and sorry, but walking quite steadily with Jim the herdsman out of the farmyard gate.

'She's all right again!' shouted Benjy, overjoyed. 'Darling! How do you feel?'

Benjy actually went out into the cold farmyard in his pyjamas and bare feet, yelling to the horse. Darling turned her big patient head.

And then an astonished voice called to him from the house. 'Benjy! What in the world do you think you are doing out there in nothing but pyjamas and bare feet! You must be mad. Come in at once!'

It was his mother—and by the tone in her voice Benjy knew she must be obeyed at once. He was in the house in a moment, grinning all over his face. 'I couldn't help it, Mother. I just had to speak to Darling. Oh, isn't it marvellous that she's better?'

'Wonderful,' said his mother. 'Everyone is as pleased as can be. Now dress quickly and see if you can eat the enormous breakfast that Harriet is keeping hot for you.'

Benjy could—and did—and when the others came home from school, what a story he had to tell them of the night before! It was just as good as a chapter out of a book.

Penny is Busy Again

February was a lovely month that year, and the four children enjoyed riding to school and back on their donkeys, doing their jobs on the farm, petting all the animals, and sometimes going joyfully off to find Tammylan, their friend.

Tammylan knew every bird and creature of the countryside, so it was marvellous to be with him. He had taught all the children to move and talk quietly when they went along the lanes, through the woods and over the hills.

'If you can learn to move as quietly as the animals do, you'll see far more and make friends with them much more easily,' he told them.

Tammylan nearly always had some animal or bird living with him in his cave. Sometimes they came to him when they were hurt, and he healed them when he could. Benjy remembered a robin with a broken leg, and a hare whose hind legs were so badly damaged that he could no longer run.

The hare had never forgotten Tammylan's kindness, and came to see the wild man almost every day. Sometimes when the children were sitting with him in his cave, they would look up to see the hare sitting at the entrance, looking inquiringly inside, his large eyes wide open, and his big ears standing straight up. At a word from Tammylan he would come inside, and the children would sit as still as mice, watching him. He would go to Benjy sometimes, but not to any other of the children.

'Well, Penny,' said Tammylan one day when the little girl had come to see him with Benjy, 'how are Davey's lambs getting along? Are you helping him with them?'

'Oh, Tammylan, isn't it bad luck for me—not one of the mother-sheep has had three lambs this year,' said Penny. 'You know, Davey the shepherd *promised* I could have another lamb for my own as soon as a sheep had three, instead of one or two. He says three is too much for a mother to manage properly. But not a single sheep has had more than two lambs. I do feel upset. I haven't any pet of my own at all now—and nothing to look after.'

'You could help Sheila with her hens and ducks,' said the wild man.

'No,' said Penny. 'She has Fanny to help her. I just stand round and watch, and I don't like that. I like to *do* something!'

Penny soon had her wish granted. When the two of them went back home, they found a great disturbance going on. Something had happened!

'What is it?' shouted Benjy, as he saw Jim running up on to the hillside where the sheep were grazing. 'Has anything happened?'

'Sheep got caught in the barbed wire up yonder!' yelled back Jim. 'Sort of hanged itself, I reckon. We're trying to save it.'

Benjy and Penny ran to join the men, who were doing their best to disentangle the sheep from the twisted strands of barbed wire. It had evidently tried to jump the ditch to join its two little lambs on the far side, and had got caught in the wire. It had struggled and struggled, and had got the wire all round its neck. It was baaing piteously.

Its two little lambs stood near by, bleating in fright. Rascal was there, preventing them from jumping into the ditch. The men worked hard with wire-clippers, cutting the wire here and there to help the sheep. One strand sprang back and cut a long, deep scratch down Jim's arm. The red blood flowed at once—but Jim did not seem even to notice it.

'Oh, poor Jim!' said Penny, in distress. She never could bear to see anyone hurt. But Jim gave her a cheerful grin.

'Never felt it!' he said. 'Don't you worry!'

At last the poor sheep was free from the cruel wire that had torn her and cut her even through her thick wool, for she had struggled so much. She tried to run a few steps over the grass, but fell down. Rascal ran to her and gently nosed her towards the waiting shepherd. Her two lambs ran up to her, bleating, for they wanted her milk—but she butted them away angrily. She was too frightened and hurt to want her lambs just then.

'I reckon she won't want to feed her lambs again,' said Jim, and Davey the shepherd nodded gloomily.

'That's so,' he said. 'She'll not have any milk for them after this scare. I'll have to try and put them to another ewe.' Then he felt a warm little hand in his and turned to see Penny's bright eyes looking up at him pleadingly.

'Davey,' she said, 'Davey! Why can't *I* have them? You promised me a lamb to feed and I haven't had one. Can't I have these two? They are so miserable—listen how they bleat. They are saying, "We want Penny to look after us! We want Penny!" '

Davey laughed. He patted Penny on the head. 'Now, now, Tuppenny,' he said, 'don't get all excited till we see what the old ewe is going to do. Maybe she'll want her lambs after all. But if she doesn't—why, then, you shall have them!'

'Oh, thank you!' cried Penny, skipping about like a lamb herself. 'I'm sure I shall have them. What shall I call them? Let me see—Frisky—Frolicky Wriggly—'

Benjy laughed just as Davey had done. 'Oh, Penny, you and your names! Come and tell Mother. We'll have to hunt out a couple of feeding-bottles if you are going to have the lambs.'

Penny went off with him happily, and Mother found two feeding-bottles, just in case they were needed in a hurry. Lambs needed many feeds when they were small, and it would not do to let the two little lambs go too long without milk.

Penny is Busy Again

Penny had her way. The mother-sheep would not even try to feed her little lambs again, and Davey brought them down to Penny that afternoon. Rascal ran round them when the shepherd set them down outside the kitchen door. He had carried them under his arms from the hillside, little, sad, bleating creatures, their whole world changed because their mother butted them away from her. Poor thing, she had had a terrible shock, and it would take her a week or two to get over it.

'It's a good thing Rascal found her when he did, and came to fetch me,' said Davey to Penny's mother, who had come out to see the lambs. 'She would have died if we hadn't cut her free, and we can't afford to lose a good ewe like that. Now, little Tuppenny—you'll be happy to have lambs again, won't you?'

Davey always called Penny Tuppenny, because he said a penny was too cheap for her. The little girl was fond of the big shepherd, with his wise blue eyes and weather-beaten face. He knew so much about his sheep —but he always said that his dogs knew even more!

Harriet filled the feeding-bottles with milk and gave them to Penny. The little girl put on the teats firmly. 'They're exactly as if they were to feed a baby, not a lamb,' said Fanny, whose mother had a new baby at home, often fed by Fanny from its bottle. 'But, my word—those lambs suck the milk more quickly than a baby does!'

The lambs were terribly hungry, poor little things. Penny went to them, and offered the smaller one the first bottle. She squeezed the teat a little so that milk came into it and the smell reached the lamb's nose. It turned towards the little girl, and it was not long before it was sucking noisily! The other one came nosing round at once, and soon Penny had the joy of feeding both the tiny creatures, a bottle in each hand.

'You won't be able to feed both at once in a few days' time!' said Benjy, watching. 'They will come rushing at you then as soon as they see you, Penny—and you'll have to feed them one at a time, and keep the other lamb off as best you can!'

What Benjy said was true. The lambs soon grew to know Penny, and even if she had no feeding-bottles full of milk with her, they would come rushing up to her eagerly, almost knocking her over. They even put their front-legs up against her waist almost as if they thought they were puppies!

Penny loved them. 'You are just every bit as sweet as the lamb I had last year,' she told the two little creatures. 'He was called Skippetty—and he *was* skippetty too! He skipped about all over the place. I shall call you Jumpity and Hoppitty, because you jump and hop all round me. Jumpity, you're the one with the black nose. Hoppitty, you're the one without.'

Soon the lambs followed Penny everywhere, and she was very happy. 'If only my birthday would hurry up and I could have the little kid that Daddy promised me!' she thought. 'Then I would have three dear little creatures of my very own. I wish lambs didn't grow into sheep and kids into goats. It does seem such a pity.'

Penny is Busy Again

Penny's birthday came at the beginning of March, and she was very excited. 'I'm going to be nine,' she told everyone. 'Then next year I shall be ten, and be in double figures. But I shall never catch up Benjy or the others.'

'Of course not,' said Mother. 'Now I wonder what I can give you for your birthday!'

When Penny's birthday came at last, she had a lovely day. Mother gave her a new mirror for her bedroom, with flowers all round it. It looked beautiful on her chest-of-drawers. Benjy gave her a pencil-box with two lambs on it that he said were exactly like Hoppitty, and Jumpity. Sheila gave her a work-box made of shells, and Rory gave her a fat little walking-stick. This pleased her very much, for she had always wanted a proper stick of her own.

Harriet made her a wonderful birthday cake with nine candles on it, and pink roses all round. It had 'A happy birthday to Penny' on it, written in pink icing in Harriet's best icing-handwriting.

Tammylan came to tea and brought Penny a very curious stone. It shone a dull blue, and in the middle of it was a twisted line in yellow, almost exactly like the letter P.

'P for Penny,' said Tammylan solemnly. 'I found it at the back of my cave, in that little spring there that wells up. Perhaps the hare brought it for you. Anyway, it's very strange and unusual, but it *must* be meant for you, because it has P on it.'

Penny was thrilled. She felt quite certain that the stone was magic, and she slipped it into her pocket at

57

once, keeping her hand on it till it grew warm. 'It's a magic stone,' she told everyone. 'Very magic. If I want anything very badly I shall hold it in my hand till it gets warm, and then I shall wish—and my wish might come true!'

The present that Penny liked best of all was from her father. He kept his promise to her—and brought her a little kid! It was snow-white with a black mark in the middle of its back. It bleated in a little high voice, and Penny loved it the moment she saw it.

'Oh!' she squealed in delight. 'Daddy, what a darling little kid! It can run about with my two lambs, can't it? Oh, I do love it. Thank you, Daddy, ever so much. Oh, what shall I call it?'

'Squealer,' said Rory.

'Sniffy,' said Sheila.

'Sooty,' said Benjy, with a laugh, fondling the kid's snow-white head. Penny looked at the others with scorn.

'You're all silly,' she said. 'I shall think of dozens of names much, much better than any you could think of!'

Penny did. She went round the house and farm-yard saying strings of names, trying to find one that would suit the little kid. The two lambs ran beside the little white creature, butting it gently with their noses. It was funny to see them.

'Snowy, Snowball, Snowdrop, Snow-white,' chanted Penny, as she went. 'No—somehow none of these names suits you, little kid. Oh, come away from those hens! They don't like you a bit!'

Penny is Busy Again

A hen turned on the kid and pecked him. The little thing bleated and jumped straight on to the top of a bin. The lid was half balanced on it and slipped off. The kid disappeared inside the bin, and Penny had to rescue him from the corn inside.

'Really!' she said. 'Whatever will you do next?' The next thing he did was to run under Blossom, one of the cart-horses, and give her such a start that she reared up. The kid leapt out from under her and fell into the duck-pond.

'There's only one name for that kid of yours, Penny,' said Fanny, with a laugh. She had come out to feed the hens. 'Call him Dopey. He's quite mad, and always will be. You can tell it from his eyes. He'll be a darling— but quite, quite mad just like the dear little dwarf Dopey in the story of Snow-white.'

'Yes—Dopey is a nice name,' said Penny. 'You shall be called Dopey, little kid. Now I've got Hoppitty, Jumpity, and Dopey. I *am* lucky! I really am!'

Penny had a wonderful time with her three pets. She fed them herself, and, as Fanny had said, little Dopey was quite, quite mad. He was maddest of all when he tried to eat things he shouldn't—from muddy shoes left out in the yard, to barbed wire round the gaps in the hedges! There was just no stopping him.

'You'll get a dreadful tummy-ache, just like Darling did once,' Penny warned him. But somehow he never did!

The Coming of the Bull

The children's father sold his store of potatoes at top prices. They were wonderful potatoes, quite untouched by the frost, and he had had a marvellous crop. He was very pleased indeed.

'I've made quite a heap of money,' he told the children. 'Now—what would be the best thing to do with it?'

That was the nice part about their father—he always told the children what was happening, and they listened and learnt a tremendous lot about profits and prices, as well as about the animals and crops themselves. As they all meant to be farmers or farmers' wives when they grew up, they took the greatest interest in what was told them.

'Daddy—what about a bull?' said Rory at once. 'We ought to have a bull. Let's buy a good one.'

'And what about new cow-sheds?' asked Benjy. 'I like our old ones—but since you said you'd like to have new ones, Daddy, I've been reading up about them. And ours really *are* old-fashioned. It would be lovely to have proper ones. Do you know, Daddy, that in some cow-sheds the cows can actually turn on their own water-tap in their drinking bowls so as to get perfectly fresh water when they want it? And, Daddy, we must have curved mangers, so that they don't get corners full of dust like ours. And …'

'Half a minute, half a minute!' laughed his father. 'My word, I've only just got to mention a thing and you've got it all at your finger-ends at once. Cow-sheds cost an awful lot of money—we'd better wait a while for those—but a bull I *could* get. Yes—I think we'll go off to market and get a bull this very week!'

This was a great thrill. The children talked of nothing else but bulls, and when Mark came to spend the day with them, they talked to him about it too.

Mark was not at all thrilled. He had hardly got over his dislike of the horns on cows, and to him a bull was a creature that ran at you and tossed you whenever you came by! He secretly hoped that there would be no bull at the market to buy. He felt that he would not enjoy coming to Willow Farm nearly so much if it had a bull.

The children were going to market with their father to get the bull that very day—so Mark went with them. They all set off on their donkeys, but Mark went with the farmer in his car, feeling rather grand—though really he would have preferred the fun of riding on a donkey.

There were three bulls at the market that day. One was a youngster, big and strong, dark brown all over. The other two were older, enormous creatures that bellowed loudly enough to set all the sheep baaing, hens clucking, ducks quacking and cows mooing. It was astonishing to hear them.

The price of the young bull was low. The children's father liked the look of him, and thought that he would live for many years as master of the herd of quiet cows. Perhaps he would be the father of many good milking-cows. Benjy was the only one of them who didn't like the bull, and he couldn't say why. Sometimes, like Tammylan, the boy sensed something and didn't know why. He just felt that the bull wasn't going to be a success.

'Well, I can't afford to pay the price of either of the other two,' said his father. 'It's a pity Tammylan isn't here. He might be able to tell me if this bull is really a good bargain. Everyone seems to think he is—so I'll risk it and buy him.'

So the bull was bought. Penny couldn't name him, for he already had a name that he knew. He was called Stamper—a good name for him because he stamped a great deal in his narrow pen, and roared to be let out.

'I should think his second name is Roarer,' said Penny, looking at him. 'Look at the ring through his nose. Mark, do you know what he wears that for?'

'So that he can be led by it, of course!' said Mark, who already knew this from Benjy. 'A bull can't do anything much if someone puts a stick through his ring—it hurts him too much if he tries to be silly and run away—or chase anyone. I say—I hope your bull doesn't chase any of *you.*'

'Of course not,' said Rory. 'It's only bulls in story-books that do that. You'll see our bull will soon settle down—and I expect Penny will try to take him lumps of sugar, just like she does Darling. I believe she would give sugar to the ducks if they'd have it!'

The bull was brought to Willow Farm that evening by the man who had reared him from a calf. He was a little man with a most enormous voice and hands as big as hams. His face was red-brown as an autumn apple, and his eyes were so blue that you simply had to look at them in astonishment. He spoke to the bull in his enormous voice, and bade him behave himself in his new home.

'Now don't you disgrace me,' boomed the little man fiercely, and he gave the bull a smack on its big head. 'You behave yourself. No monkey-tricks! No nonsense —or I'll be after you, so I will.'

The bull backed a little away from the fierce little man, and blinked at him. The man gave the ring in the bull's nose a little pull by way of farewell.

'I hope the next I hear of you is that you are the proud father of many beautiful calves!' he said. 'Well—good-bye, Stamper. I'm sorry to part with you!'

He was paid his price and went away, calling back to the bull as he went.

'Now see you behave yourself, Stamper—I'll be after you if you don't!'

The children thought all this was very funny indeed. Jim took the bull to the little paddock where he was to live. He led him in and shut the stout gate. The bull gave a mild roar, and stamped round a bit. Penny sat on the gate watching him.

'You come down from there, Missy,' said Jim. 'That bull feels strange tonight, in a new home. He might tip you off.'

'Oh, do come down, Penny,' begged Mark, who was still with the children. 'You'd just hate to be tossed.'

Penny didn't get down. She really didn't feel afraid of the bull, and she felt sure he liked her. But he didn't. He didn't like anything that night. He hadn't liked the strange market. He hadn't liked walking to Willow Farm. And now he didn't like that little girl on his gate.

'Wooooooorrrrrr!' he roared suddenly and stamped loudly. He lowered his head and looked under his eyelids at Penny. Then he made a rush for the gate, his horns lowered ready to toss.

Rory just managed to pull Penny down in time. The bull crashed into the gate and got such a shock that he stood still, glaring round him.

'Penny, you really are a little idiot!' said Rory, angry and frightened. 'Daddy will forbid us all to go near the bull if you behave in this silly, foolish way. You might have been gored by his horns.'

Penny looked a bit white. She had got so used to farm life and to all the creatures, big and little, welcoming her, that it was a shock to her to find that the bull had been about to hurt her.

'I won't be silly again, Rory,' she said quickly. 'Don't tell tales of me. I promise not to sit on the bull's gate again.'

Benjy was the only one who didn't like the bull, and he couldn't say why.

'He looked quite mad when he rushed at you,' said Benjy. 'Really, I don't like him a bit. I hope he soon settles down and gets used to us. Some bulls get quite tame.'

Stamper did settle down after a few days. He seemed to like his paddock, and curiously enough he always welcomed Hoppitty, Jumpity and Dopey when they squeezed through a little hole and came to visit him. He would trot up to them and make a curious noise in his throat to welcome them. They would all three frisk round him madly, and he would pretend to chase them, his great powerful head lowered. But he never did them any harm at all, and Penny soon stopped being afraid that he would toss them over the gate.

The only time he ever got annoyed with the two lambs and little kid was when they came into his paddock one day when he was lying down, and Dopey actually began to nibble his tail. Dopey, of course, would eat anything he came across, but he should have thought twice before he tried to eat the tail of a bull. Stamper leapt up with a bellow and chased the three swiftly round the paddock. They squeezed out in fright and didn't go near Stamper for two days. But when they did go he had quite forgotten his annoyance and gave them a great welcome.

Everyone grew used to Stamper. Nobody bothered about his roaring. He seemed to like the cows, and was just about as good and sensible a bull as could be. He grazed peacefully in the orchard, on the watch for the two lambs and the kid, and he no longer minded if any of the children climbed up on the gate.

'He isn't the tiniest *bit* fierce,' said Penny. 'Honestly, Benjy, I believe I could teach him to nibble a carrot or a lump of sugar.'

'Well, don't you try,' said Benjy, who still did not trust Stamper, though he felt rather silly about this, and could not imagine why he did not like the bull. Usually Benjy liked every animal, and because they felt that, they trusted him and came to him. But Stamper would never come to Benjy.

'He was a good bargain,' said the farmer, when he passed Stamper's paddock. 'We did well to choose him. He's settling down fine.'

But he spoke too soon. When the warmer days came, Stamper became very restless. He roared a great deal and galloped savagely round his paddock. The men soon began to dislike to go in there.

'He's going mad!' said Jim. 'Look at the whites of his eyes showing. He's going mad! We'll have to look out.'

A Nasty Accident

That springtime there came some very heavy gales. The children awoke in the mornings and saw the trees outside bending their heads in the wind, and at night they heard the howling of the gale round the old farmhouse.

At first they all liked the wind and the sound it made. 'It's a bit like the sea, really,' said Rory.

'It's exciting, I think,' said Penny. 'I like to run out in the wind and feel it pulling my hair back almost as if it had fingers!'

But after the wind had howled without stopping for three or four days, everyone became very tired of it. 'It gets inside my head,' complained Sheila.

'I shall go mad if someone doesn't keep the dairy door shut, to stop it banging,' said Mother.

'Look at my ankle,' said Rory, pulling down his sock. 'The lid blew off the corn-bin this morning and it simply *raced* across the yard, and met me just round a corner. Look at the bruise I got!'

'Scamper's tired of the wind too,' said Benjy, putting up his hand to stroke his squirrel, who was nestling on his shoulder. 'It blew him over sideways yesterday when he went across that windswept bit of ground up by the orchard.'

A Nasty Accident

The wind grew wilder that night. It seemed to grow a voice of its own. It bellowed down the big chimneys and shook and rattled every door and window in the house.

Nobody could sleep. They lay in their beds and listened to the howling of the gale. The farmer was worried. He wondered if the roof of the cow-shed was safe. He wondered if any trees would fall.

And then, in the middle of the night, there came a curious sound. It was like a very large creaking at first, mixed with a kind of sighing. Then there came an extra large creak and a long-drawn-out crash. Then silence.

Everyone sat up in bed. 'What's that?' asked Penny in fright.

'Don't know,' said Sheila. She pattered across to Rory's room. He was awake too. 'Rory, did you hear that? What was it?'

'A tree falling,' said Rory. He and Sheila went to the window and looked out into the dark, wind-blown night. But they could see nothing at all. They couldn't imagine which tree it was. It must have been a big one, that was certain.

In the morning Jim came knocking early at the farmhouse door. The farmer opened it. He was having his early morning cup of tea.

'There's a tree down, sir,' said Jim. 'It's the big elm over beyond the cow-sheds. It's caught itself in the next tree, so the sheds are safe. But I reckon we'd better do something about it soon, in case it slips and knocks in the shed roof. It's a mercy it didn't hit the sheds. It would have given the cows a nasty shock, if it had.'

The farmer hurried to see the damage. It looked a strange sight. A big elm, rotten at the roots, had not been able to stand against the gale. It had not been broken in half, but had simply been uprooted and had fallen. Instead of falling on to the cow-sheds, which were near, it had crashed into another elm, which had just saved it from breaking down the sheds with its topmost branches.

'We'd better get Bill here and he and I must get to work to lop up the old tree before it does any more damage,' said Jim. 'I can climb up into the second elm, there, and saw the topmost branches of the fallen tree out of it. Then Bill and I can tackle the rest of the tree between us. It will mean a waste of time, and we're busy enough in the fields just now—but anyway, there'll be plenty of logs this winter.'

The children all went to look at the half-fallen tree, on their way to school. They danced their donkeys round and round it, exclaiming at the sight. 'It might have smashed in the sheds!'

'It might have killed half the cows!'

'No wonder it made a noise. It's a simply enormous tree, the biggest on the farm I should think!'

The farmer came up, rubbing his cheek as he always did when he was troubled. 'If that other tree hadn't been there, things might have been serious,' he said. 'As it is, we'll lose a few days' work, have some extra trouble —but plenty of good wood for the winter fires!'

The children hurried home that day to see how Bill and Jim had got on with the fallen tree. Both men were up in the tree next to it, sawing away hard. They had already managed to saw off many of the topmost branches, and these lay on the ground. Scamper ran along them inquisitively.

The children stood and watched. The fallen tree had broken many of the branches of the tree next to it. It seemed to Rory as if that tree had been pushed a little sideways!

He stood looking at it. Yes—it really did seem as if it was leaning over a little. He was sure it had been quite straight up before.

'Don't you think the fallen tree has pushed its neighbour over a bit?' he said to Benjy. Benjy looked too. Then he looked again.

'Rory,' he said, 'I think it's moving now, this very minute! I think it's going to fall!'

The children stared, their eyes wide. Surely it wasn't moving. But then it gave a slight creak.

Rory yelled to the men in the tree. 'Your tree's going to fall! The other one's pushing it over. Get out, quick!'

'It won't fall,' said Bill, still busy sawing. 'It would have fallen before, if it was going to.'

There came another creak. Rory jumped violently. He was very anxious. 'Bill! Jim! You *must* come down! I know your tree is going to fall, I know it is!'

Scamper took a look up at the tree and then fled away, his tail streaming out behind him. He smelt danger.

Bill stopped sawing. Another creak came, and he scratched his head. He didn't for one moment think

71

there was any danger, but he reckoned he'd better go down and see what was worrying Rory. There might be danger for the children.

So down he swung, slipping easily from bough to bough, landing with a jump on to the ground. 'Now,' he said, with a grin, 'let's see what all the fuss is about!'

There came such a creak that it sounded almost like a groan—and before everyone's eyes the tree that Bill had just left slipped a good bit sideways. Half its roots came out of the ground. Bill gave a terrified yell.

'Jim! Come on down! The tree's going to fall. Get out of the way, children. Run! Quick!'

The four children ran. Rory caught hold of Penny's hand and pulled her along fast. She almost fell over. Behind them came enormous creaks and groans as the tree heaved itself out of the ground.

'Oh, is Jim all right, is Jim all right?' cried Penny. She was very fond of Jim, who was never too busy to talk to her. 'Is he out of the tree?'

The children stopped and turned, when they were well away from the tree. It was a strange sight they saw. The fallen elm's weight had been too much for its neighbour and now the second tree was falling too. Over it went, as the children watched in terror. It fell slowly, so slowly—and caught in its big branches was poor Jim, who had had no time to save himself!

Everyone watched in fear, trying to see where Jim was. He gave a shout as the tree fell. It reached the ground with a terrific crash and then settled itself there as if it meant to go to sleep. Its neighbour lay on top of it, and their branches were tangled and mixed so that one could not be told from the other. The trees seemed enormous as they lay there on the ground. They just missed the cow-sheds, though some of the lighter branches struck the roof, doing no damage.

'Jim! Where are you, Jim?' cried Bill, and he ran at once to the tree. The children's father and mother came running up too, for they had heard the crash. Harriet came and Fanny, and even Davey the shepherd hurried down from the hillside.

There was no answering cry from Jim. There was no movement of someone scrambling out of the tree. The farmer waved the children back, as they ran up to the trees.

'You're not to come near,' he said. He was afraid that Jim might have been killed, and he did not want the children to see the poor fellow.

All the grown-ups began to scramble over the spreading, fallen branches, trying to get into the middle of the tree, where Jim had been. The farmer shouted to Sheila.

'Sheila! Better go and ring up the doctor and tell him to come at once. We'll need him when we get Jim.'

Sheila sped off, and Penny went with her, crying from fright and anxiety. It had all happened so suddenly. She could hardly believe it!

The farmer soon found Jim. He was lying in the middle of the tree, his eyes closed, and a great, bleeding bruise on his head.

'Careful now,' said the farmer, as he and the others gently lifted poor Jim out. 'Careful! He may have a leg or arm broken.'

73

Jim was laid on the ground, and the children's mother examined him anxiously. 'He doesn't seem to have any limbs broken,' she said. 'I think it's just his head. He must have been knocked unconscious when the tree fell. Get some water, Harriet, and I'll see how bad this bruise is.'

The doctor was in when Sheila telephoned, and as soon as he heard what the matter was he jumped into his car and came round at once. He was soon bending over Jim, feeling his body here and there.

'Will he be all right?' asked the farmer.

'There's not much wrong,' said the doctor cheerfully. 'He got a knock on the head from the trunk or a branch. That knocked him out properly. He's got concussion, and he'll have to be kept quiet for a bit. Put him off work for a week or ten days, then he'll be as right as rain!'

Everyone was glad to know that Jim was not seriously hurt. Davey and Bill carried him back to his cottage, and his wife put him to bed. He had not opened his eyes.

'He may not come to himself for a while,' said the doctor. 'Let him be. He's a strong fellow and it won't be long before he's himself again.'

'I wish I hadn't let him go up into that tree,' said the farmer that evening. 'Elms are dangerous trees. They go rotten at the roots, and then, in a storm, they suddenly get top-heavy and fall. I might have guessed that that second elm was rotten too.'

'I shall go and see Jim every day and take him one of my books to read,' said Penny. 'It will be quite a holiday for him, won't it, Daddy?'

'Yes,' said her father. 'But unluckily this has come at one of our busiest times of year, when I need Jim out in the fields all day long. And there's the milk-round too. I can't see how I can possibly spare Bill for that. He's not good at things like that, either. He'll probably get into a frightful muddle, and charge all the bills wrong.'

'Daddy! Oh, Daddy! Can't Rory and I do the milk-round whilst Jim is ill?' cried Benjy eagerly. 'Ebony's so good, Jim says she already knows half the houses she has to stop at.'

'You can't do the milk-round,' said the farmer, half laughing. 'There's more in it than simply taking bottles of milk and standing them on door-steps! You have to keep the milk-book very carefully too, and enter up everything in it.'

'Well, Rory is awfully good at that sort of thing,' said Benjy earnestly. 'He's the best at maths in our little school. I could give out the milk and drive, and Rory could do the money part.'

'I don't see why they shouldn't try,' said Mother suddenly. 'It would save you a good deal if they could do that, wouldn't it? You wouldn't need to take Bill from his field-work then. Let them try just once. If they don't do it properly, *I'll* do it!'

'No, you won't, Mother!' cried Rory. 'Benjy and I will manage beautifully. We shall have to be late for school each day, that's all.'

'All right—you can try,' said their father, with a laugh. 'Begin tomorrow. You'll have to harness Ebony into the cart, get the milk and everything. Bill can give you a hand tomorrow, and then we'll see how you get on!'

The Two New Milkmen

The boys were really excited about their milk-round. They felt very grown up. They fetched Jim's books and had a look at them. In the books were entered the name and address of every customer, the amount of milk they took each day, and what was paid. There were some 'standing orders'—that meant that the same amount of milk was to be left each day. Those would be easy to do.

'I know what we'll do tonight,' said Benjy. 'I'll copy out the names and addresses on a big sheet of paper, and we'll pin it in the cart, so that we don't have to keep on and on looking up the books. Jim knows everyone by heart, because he does the round so often, but we don't. We shall waste an awful lot of time if we keep having to look up the names.'

So that was done, and a big sheet was soon ready for the next day. Then Rory made out a list of the 'standing orders' so that those could be dealt with easily in the same way. It was fun. They felt important.

'We'd better begin at this street,' said Rory, pointing to an address on the list.

'No,' said Benjy. 'We'll begin here, look. We don't want to overlap the streets at all. We want to deliver the milk and go the shortest distance to do it.'

But it wasn't any good planning *that*! Ebony had her own ideas about which was the best way to go! She took charge of the milk round, as the boys soon found out.

They were up early the next morning. They went out to the sheds, where Bill, Harriet and Fanny were already milking the cows. It was cooled, and put into the waiting bottles, which had been cleaned and sterilised the day before.

'Well, roundsmen?' said Harriet, a twinkle in her eye. 'Ready for your work?'

'We're going straightaway, as soon as the milk's in the bottles,' said Rory.

'Not going to stop for anything?' said Fanny.

'No,' said Rory.

'Dear me, what a pity!' said Harriet. 'Jim always stopped for a cup of cocoa and a slice of cake before he set off.'

'Oh, well—we could stop for *that*,' said Rory, with a laugh. So, when the bottles were all ready, and the boys were setting them carefully in the racks in their milk-cart, Fanny was sent off to the kitchen for the cocoa and the cake. The two roundsmen ate and drank quickly, for they were anxious to be off.

'We shan't be so quick as Jim was, at first,' said Rory. 'He knew everyone to go to and we don't. But we shall soon learn. Now—let's get Ebony. You fetch her, Benjy.'

Benjy went off to get the little horse. Ebony looked at him out of her gentle eyes, rather astonished to see Benjy, instead of Jim. But, like all the horses, she loved Benjy, and whinnied softly as he took her out to the cart. He harnessed her and then rubbed her soft nose.

'Now, Ebony! *We're* the milkmen today! So off you go, and show us the right houses to call at!'

The milk was sold to four or five villages around. Ebony set off at a canter, dragging the little milk-cart easily behind her. Benjy drove, his lean brown hands holding the leather reins loosely.

'Let's go to Tittleton first,' said Rory, looking up from the list he was studying.

'Right,' said Benjy, and when he came to the road that forked to Tittleton, he pulled on the rein to make Ebony go the right way.

Ebony took no notice at all! She just tossed her brown head, and took the other way, cantering steadily along!

'Ebony!' yelled Benjy, pulling at the rein. 'You're going the wrong way!'

The little horse stopped. She looked round inquiringly, gazed at the milk-bottles, said 'Hrrrumph' softly and set off down the road again, taking her own way!

Benjy began to laugh. He let her go the way she wanted. 'Rory, isn't she funny?' he said. 'Did you see how she stopped and looked round at the milk-bottles? Then she thought to herself, "Well, there the bottles are, as usual, so I must be right. Off I go!" And off she went!'

'Better let her go the way she wants to,' said Rory, with a grin. 'We'll see where she takes us to. She's a clever little thing.' She was! She cantered smartly into the nearest village and came to a stop outside a house called 'Green Gates.'

'Quite right, Ebony,' said Rory, laughing. 'Green Gates. Standing order, two pints of milk. Here you are, Benjy. Leave it on the door-step.'

Benjy jumped down, took the quart of milk, sped in with it, dumped it down on the step and ran out again. Almost before he was in the cart, Ebony was cantering down the quiet street, coming to a stop before a row of little houses.

A woman came out. She was surprised to see two boys instead of Jim. 'Pint, please,' she said, 'and here's the money.'

'Are you Mrs Jones?' asked Rory, and he put a tick against the woman's name and wrote down the money she had given him. Benjy gave her the milk. Ebony took a few steps on, and stopped again, at No. 10.

'Standing order, one pint,' said Rory, and Benjy hopped out again. Whilst he was out, Ebony moved on again, missing out three houses and stopping at the fourth. It was No. 18.

'Golly, isn't Ebony clever?' said Rory, looking at the list. 'You're right, Ebony. No. 18 is the next customer!'

The little horse knew the milk-round just as well as Jim did. She knew where to stop, and Benjy felt certain that if she could speak she would tell him whether to leave a pint of milk, or two or three! She turned her head each time to watch the boys take the bottles.

'Just as if she was watching to see if we were taking the right amount!' said Rory.

Then off to the next village they went at a canter. Ebony was just as good there. Once the boys could not see where a house called 'Top Wood' was. Ebony stood outside the gate, but when the boys went through it, they could see no house.

Ebony whinnied to them as if she wanted to tell them something. They came back to the gate. Ebony suddenly left the roadway and walked up to the gate with the cart. She went through it and then went a little way up a small dark path the boys had not noticed.

'Oh. That must be the way, not the other path, I suppose,' said Benjy. And he was right. The first path, the wrong one, led to a workshop belonging to the little house, which was built among trees and hard to see. It was reached by the little path that Ebony had shown the boys.

The milk-round was easy with Ebony to help them so much. The horse really seemed to think. She seemed to know that the boys were new at the job and wanted help. It was difficult sometimes when a house had only a name, not a number, to know exactly where it was. But Ebony always knew.

'Oh dear—where's Cherry Trees?' sighed Benjy. 'It's got no number, and not even a street. It must be one of those houses standing by itself.'

'Cherry Trees, Ebony!' called Rory. And, as if she quite understood, Ebony would trot over to a house, and there on the gate would be the right name—Cherry Trees! It did make things easy.

'We shall know much better tomorrow,' said Rory, marking down the money he had been given at Cherry Trees. 'It is really rather fun, isn't it, Benjy? Now we know the history of our milk from when it leaves the cow to when it reaches the people who make it into custards and puddings!'

They were tired when the round was finished. Ebony cantered home at a smart pace, and the boys waved to their father when they met him in the road beyond the farm.

'How did you get on?' he called.

'Fine!' cried Rory. 'Ebony knows everything. *She* did the milk-round, not us! How's Jim, do you know?'

'He's much better,' said their father. 'I've been in to see him. He's come out of that faint he was in. He says he's got an awful headache, but that will pass. Nobody is to see him till tomorrow, except me. Then tomorrow you can go and tell him how you got on with the milk-round!'

The boys gave their mother the lists of money they had taken, and told her about Ebony. She gave them a good breakfast and then told them to get their donkeys and hurry off to school. 'You'll be tired at the end of the morning!' she said. 'You'll be wanting *me* to do the milk-round tomorrow.'

'We shan't!' said Benjy stoutly. Mother was right when she said they would be tired. They were. But it made no difference to their feelings about the milk-round. They were going to do it just as long as Jim was ill. And they were going to do it properly too.

So they were up early again the next morning, seeing about the milk, harnessing Ebony to the cart, and setting off in the early morning sunshine. But it rained before they got back and they were wet through. That wasn't so pleasant. The wind was cold, and the boys were chilled when they got back to their breakfast, very hungry and wet.

'Change your wet things,' said Mother. 'Yes, at once, before you have your breakfast, please. I don't want to have you in bed as well as Jim! We'd have to get Penny and Scamper to do the milk-round then.'

It was pouring with rain the next day too when the boys set off. The milk-round did not seem quite so jolly. The boys said very little as they set off in the cart.

'This is beastly, isn't it?' said Benjy, pulling his collar up to stop the rain falling down his neck. 'I don't feel at all excited about the milk-round today!'

'Nor do I,' said Rory honestly. 'But we've got to stick it, and stick it without grumbling, Benjy. We took it on and we've got to keep it going all right.'

'Of course!' said Benjy. 'Get on, Ebony! We'll be as quick as we can today.'

For a whole week the two boys did the milk-round between them. They soon knew almost as well as Ebony did what customers to serve and what houses to stop at. The little horse worked in very well with the boys, and enjoyed their company.

Jim got rapidly better. The great lump on his head went down, and healed beautifully. Penny kept her word and took one of her books for him to read each day. Sheila and the others laughed at her.

'Fancy taking Jim books like yours!' they said. 'He doesn't want to read books about dolls and toys and things, Penny!'

But Jim thanked Penny solemnly, and said he enjoyed the books immensely, and certainly when the children went in to see him he always had one of the books open on his bed.

'It's real kind of you to do the milk-round for me and save Bill the trouble,' Jim said to the two boys. 'It means he can get on in the fields, and there's a mighty lot to do there now!'

'Oh, we like doing it!' said Rory. 'And as a matter of fact, Ebony does most of it! We never bother to guide her to the customers—she always knows them and goes there by herself. She's wonderful!'

'Yes, she was a good bargain,' said Jim. 'I'll be glad to handle the little thing again tomorrow. I miss my milk-round! I lie here thinking of all the things I ought to be doing, and it worries me.'

'Did you say you were going to do the round tomorrow?' asked Rory. He couldn't help feeling a little bit glad! 'Are you sure you'll be well enough?'

'Doctor says so,' said Jim. 'And I'm just spoiling to be at my work again. But I don't want to rob you of any pleasure—if you want to go on with my milk-round, you just say so, and I'll speak the word to your father. Though I reckon he wouldn't want you to be missing an hour's school each morning, as you've had to do!'

But Rory and Benjy did not ask Jim to speak to their father! They were glad to have had the chance of doing the round, and had enjoyed the change—but they were quite ready to give it up now Jim was better!

'Thanks, boys,' said their father that day. 'You've helped a lot. It hasn't been pleasant, I know, when the rain poured down on your open cart—but you've stuck it well, and I'm proud of you! I shall know who to turn to, another time!'

The boys glowed with pride. They went to give Ebony some lumps of sugar. 'You did most of it!' said Benjy, patting the big brown head. 'Thanks, Ebony! You're a very good sort!'

'Hrrrrumph!' said Ebony, and crunched up the sugar lumps in delight.

What Can be Done with Stamper?

Jim went to complain about the bull to the farmer. 'You should come and see him today,' he told him. 'He's just as mad as can be. There's no doing anything with him. None of us dares to go into the orchard—only those three little things of Miss Penny's go in and out still— and I'm afraid for them too.'

'Well, you'd better wire up the gap they squeeze through,' said the farmer. 'I'll go and see Stamper for myself.'

The children's father was not afraid of any animal at all. He went to the bull's paddock and had a look at him. Stamper was lying down quietly in the far corner. He did not even turn his head to look at the farmer. Wandering beside him were Hoppitty, Jumpity and Dopey, butting one another and playing touch-you-last in the funny way they had.

The farmer felt certain that Jim was exaggerating. Stamper looked as peaceful as any old cow.

'I'll go in and speak to him,' the farmer thought. 'I don't believe he'll even get up!'

What Can be Done with Stamper?

So he sprang over the gate and went into the paddock—but as he approached the bull, Stamper rose slowly to his feet. He turned to face the farmer, and showed the whites of his eyes in a curious fashion. Then he gave a bellow, lowered his head, and rushed straight at the startled man. The farmer only just had time to dodge. The bull's horns ripped a little bit out of the edge of his coat. The farmer knew then that he was in grave danger. He glanced at the gate—if only he were nearer!

Jim was passing by and he caught sight of the farmer in the paddock with the roaring bull. He ran at once to the gate.

'He's mad, sir, he's mad!' he yelled. 'Yes, he's roaring mad. You come on out, sir, or he'll toss you!'

The bull saw Jim and turned to bellow at him. The farmer edged round nearer to the gate. The bull turned again at once and pounded over the grass. He would most certainly have gored the farmer and tossed him, if something had not happened.

Little Dopey, the kid, thinking that the bull was having a kind of game, ran between his legs with an excited bleat. The bull stumbled and almost fell. That one moment gave the farmer a chance to get to the gate. He was over it and safe on the other side even as the bull was tearing up to the gate, landing against it with a crash.

The farmer fell off the gate and rolled on the ground. Jim helped him up. 'He hasn't hurt you, sir, has he?' he asked anxiously. 'What did I tell you? He's mad! He's just gone right off his head. He'll be no use to us at all. Nobody will dare to tend him now.'

'Oh, look!' said the farmer, and Jim turned to look at the bull. Poor little Dopey hadn't known that the bull was in a raging temper and he had run around him once more, bleating playfully. Stamper, furiously bellowing, lowered his huge head, got the little kid on his horns and tossed him high over the hedge.

The two men saw the snow-white kid sailing through the air, bleating in the greatest surprise. He landed in a big blackberry bush, and scrambled out as best he could.

'He's not been gored,' said Jim, looking at the frightened little creature. 'He's been scared out of his wits—not that he's got many! But he's not hurt. Those little things are like cats—they always fall on their feet. I wish the lambs would come out. They'll get tossed next.'

The lambs heard Dopey's frightened bleating and decided that it was time to escape from the paddock before they were sent flying through the air too. So they squeezed out and joined Dopey, who, with many high bleats, told them exactly what he thought of bulls.

The two men stood and looked at the mad bull. Stamper was now rushing round the paddock, tossing any old bough or log that was in his way. What was to be done with him?

'Hallo, Daddy!' came a voice behind them. 'What's happened to Stamper? He's in a fine old rage, isn't he?'

The farmer turned and saw Benjy, with Tammylan beside him. The wild man was looking intently at the bull, a troubled expression on his face.

What Can be Done with Stamper?

'Why, Tammylan!' cried Benjy's father, delighted to see the wild man. 'Can you do anything with our new bull? He seems to have gone completely mad.'

'You'll never do anything with him,' said Tammylan. 'He's a bad bargain.'

'Well, I'll have to get rid of him then,' said the farmer. 'Can't keep him here with all these children about. And anyway, the men wouldn't handle him. He'll be no use. But who *can* handle him? And what can I do with him?'

'Where did you buy him? Who sold him to you?' asked Tammylan. The farmer told him.

'Well, there is only one man who will be able to handle that bull and make him come to heel,' said Tammylan. 'And that's the man who brought him up from a calf. The bull will still remember him, and how he had to obey him—and maybe he'll go off with him like a lamb. You know, great fully-grown lions can be handled perfectly easily by a trainer who has had them as cubs. They remember the words of command and the discipline they had as cubs, and even when they are fully grown they still remember and have a respect for that man.'

'Well—I'd better telephone to Farley then,' said the farmer. 'That's the man who sold him to me. Maybe he can tell me who had the bull as a calf, and I could get him along here. But goodness knows if I can ever sell the bull now.'

The farmer went indoors to telephone. He was feeling rather miserable to think he had wasted so much money on a bull who was no good.

'Still, that's the way of farming,' he thought to himself, as he looked up the number he wanted to ring. 'You have to take the good with the bad!'

Mr Farley was in. He listened to the tale of the mad bull, and was sorry to hear it. 'Well, sir,' he said, 'I'm right sorry he was a bad bargain. But I'll tell you what I'll do for you. I'll take him back again—and give you half the price you paid for him. I can manage him all right and maybe he'll behave with me. He's of good stock, and I'll find some use for him.'

'Did you handle him as a calf?' asked the farmer.

'I did so!' answered Mr Farley. 'Ah, he'll remember me all right, the rascal. Many's the scolding I've given him for checking me! Well—will you take half-price for him, sir?'

'I'll be glad to,' said the farmer, pleased to think that he need not lose all the money he had paid. 'Thanks, Mr Farley. When shall we see you?'

'I'll be along after tea,' said Mr Farley. 'I'll come on my bike, and maybe one of your lads can bring it back for me later. I'll walk the bull home.'

The farmer was amazed. Walk the bull home! Walk mad, roaring, furious Stamper along the road, home! Why, surely no one could do that? Wouldn't it be too dangerous to allow Mr. Farley to take the bull out? He would surely be tossed high into the air.

Mr Farley arrived on his bike after tea, his blue eyes twinkling in his red-brown face. He shouted as soon as he arrived, and his enormous voice boomed round the farmyard.

'Where's that bull?'

What Can be Done with Stamper?

Everyone came hurrying out to him. Penny thought he must be the bravest man in the world. She had heard how poor Dopey had been tossed over the hedge, and had made such a fuss of the little kid that he would now hardly leave her side.

'The bull's in the paddock over there,' said the farmer. Everyone went up to the paddock. Stamper was lying down but he got up and bellowed as soon as he saw the little company coming.

'You children are to stand right away,' ordered their father. 'Rory, take Penny's hand, and don't let her go.'

'No, don't, Rory,' said Penny, trying to pull her hand away. 'I'm nine now. Don't hold my hand.'

But Rory did. He had an idea that if Dopey or the lambs went too near the bull, Penny would go after them to rescue them—and he wasn't going to have her leave his side. So Penny had to be content to leave her small hand inside Rory's big one.

Mr Farley swung himself lightly over the gate. Stamper stared in surprise at this daring fellow. He bellowed loudly.

Mr Farley had a voice that bellowed too! He yelled at the bull. 'STAMPER! You wicked fellow! How dare you behave like this? I'm ashamed of you, right down ashamed of you! Don't you remember how I scolded you when you weren't as high as my shoulder? Now just you listen to me—and don't you roar at me, either!'

The bull had run a few steps towards Mr Farley, his head lowered as if to toss him. But at the sound of the man's voice something stirred in his memory. Yes—that was the voice of the man he had known when he was a little bull-calf. He had respected that man. He had had to do as he was told with that man. He had been scolded if he hadn't obeyed. Stamper paused, remembering.

'You be careful, sir,' called Jim, who felt perfectly certain that Mr Farley was as mad as the bull. To go into that paddock without even a pitchfork in his hands—well, well, a man was mad to do that!

Mr Farley took not the slightest notice. He actually went right up to the bull! Stamper couldn't make it out at all. He stood looking at Mr Farley, his eyes rolling.

'Yes, you roll your eyes at me!' roared Mr Farley, shaking his fist at the enormous creature. 'That won't do you any good. I'm going to take you back home again. Ashamed of you, I am!'

The bull made as if he would butt Mr Farley. But the man did not budge. Instead, he caught the bull's horns in his enormous hands and shook hard. It was a tussle between the man and the bull, with Mr Farley doing the bellowing!

'Look at that now, look at that!' cried Jim beside himself with admiration and delight. 'I never saw such a sight before! Go it, Mr. Farley, sir, go it!'

Everyone was thrilled, but Mr Farley took not the slightest notice. All his attention was on his bull. He had no fear at all, and to him the big bull was simply the obstinate little bull-calf he had trained from babyhood. And, to the bull, Mr Farley was the man who had seen to him, fed him, scolded him, fussed him—and punished him.

'Now, don't you dare struggle with me, Stamper!' cried Mr Farley, and he gave the bull a firm tap on his

'Now don't you dare to struggle with me, Stamper!'
cried Mr Farley.

tough head. The bull hardly felt it, but it made him remember that he had learned discipline when he was small. He shook his head slightly and stopped rolling his eyes.

Mr Farley slipped a stick through the ring in the bull's nose. He then spoke to him firmly. 'Now we're going to walk back home. And ashamed I am to be taking you, you great unruly creature! If you so much as bellow at me I'll give you a scolding you'll remember to your dying day! Do you hear me?'

The bull heard. He looked meekly at Mr Farley. The man walked him to the gate, and everyone scattered at once. Rory dragged Penny into the barn and shut the door. She was very much annoyed.

'You can look out of the window, Penny,' said Rory. So she did, and saw the amazing sight of Mr Farley and the bull walking through the farmyard together; Mr Farley holding the big bull firmly by the ring in his nose, talking to him at the top of his enormous voice.

Even when they got to the lane everyone could still hear Mr Farley. 'A great bull like you behaving like that! What do you think you're up to? Bringing you home in disgrace like this! Sure, I'm ashamed of you I am!'

The noise of the big voice died away. The children, their father and the farm-hands rejoined one another. They were all smiling.

'As good as a play!' said the farmer. 'Well, we were lucky to get rid of a mad bull so easily. Thank goodness, Tammylan gave me the tip to get the man who'd reared Stamper from a calf! Well—that was a bit of bad luck, choosing a bull like that. Never mind—we'll know better another time.'

Everyone was glad that Stamper was gone. Nobody missed him except Dopey and the lambs. They wandered in and out of the bull's paddock quite unhappy, seeking their lost friend.

'Dopey's very forgiving,' said Penny. 'If Stamper was still there, he'd go and play with him.'

'That's because he's stupid,' said Benjy, with a laugh, and ran off before Penny could catch him and pummel him with her small fists!

Rory Wants a Dog

'You know,' said Rory, one day, 'we've none of us ever had a dog of our own. Isn't that strange? To think how fond we all are of animals—and yet we've never had a dog! I know Davey's got three—but they're not really ours, though they come to the farmyard often enough.'

'Well, let's ask Daddy if we can have a dog,' said Penny eagerly. 'A nice little puppy-dog called—called—let me see—called …'

'Oh, Penny, let's get the dog before you find a name for it,' said Rory. So they asked their father at breakfast-time the next day. But he shook his head.

'Three dogs are enough,' he said. 'We don't need any more. Anyway, we've enough cats to make up for any amount of dogs!'

That was true. There were dozens of cats about—or so it seemed! At first Penny had been sure she knew them all, but now she felt she didn't. Kittens appeared in the stables and in the barns, and she loved them and tried to pet them. But they were wild little things, and spat and scratched. Harriet had a cat of her own who lived sedately in the kitchen. He was called Mr By-Himself, because he wouldn't mix with the stable cats.

'But, Daddy, a dog is worth a dozen cats,' said Rory. 'I'd so love a dog of my own.'

'Well, we'll see,' said Daddy. 'If I hear of a good puppy, I'll perhaps get it for you.'

But Daddy didn't seem to hear of one—and it was Benjy who produced a dog after all for Rory! He was going down the lane one day, whistling softly to himself, Scamper on his shoulder, when he thought he heard a little whine from somewhere. Benjy stopped. Scamper leapt down from his shoulder and went to hunt around in the ditch. He found something there and leapt back to Benjy's shoulder, making tiny barking noises in his ear, as if to say, 'Come and see, come and see!'

Benjy went to the ditch and parted the nettles there. Lying among them was a dog, his brown eyes looking beseechingly up at the boy.

'What's the matter?' said Benjy. 'Are you hurt?'

The dog whined. Benjy stamped down the nettles that stung his hands and legs, and tried to lift up the dog. It was a mongrel dog, rather like a rough-haired terrier.

You've been run over!' said Benjy pityingly. 'Poor creature! I'll carry you home.'

Benjy knew that it was dangerous to touch hurt animals, for they will turn on anyone, even their owner. But animals always loved the boy, and he was never afraid of them. The dog allowed him to carry it in his arms, and he went down the lane with it, Scamper on his shoulder, peering down at the hurt animal in his bright, inquisitive way.

97

Benjy took the dog to Rory. 'Rory! Look at this poor hurt dog! Wouldn't you like to have it for your own? I'm sure Daddy wouldn't say no.'

'But it must already belong to someone!' said Rory. 'Oh, Benjy—it's bleeding. I'll get a bowl of water and a rag.'

Rory bathed the dog, which allowed him to do everything, though once or twice it bared its teeth when Rory accidentally hurt it. Rory liked the dog immensely. It licked his hands, and the boy's heart warmed to it. Benjy liked the dog too, but he wanted Rory to have it. He knew how much his brother longed for a pet of his own. After all, he had Scamper.

Their mother and father were out. The two boys made the dog as comfortable as they could, and gave it water to drink. Penny, Sheila and Fanny came to look at it, and they all thought it was a darling.

'Its eyes look at you so gratefully, Rory,' said Penny. 'It keeps on and on looking at you. I'm sure it loves you.'

Rory was sure it did too. When he went to bed that night he put the hurt dog in a basket in his bedroom. His father and mother had still not come back, and he felt that he really must have the dog near him. He hoped his mother wouldn't mind.

Next day he showed the dog to his mother. 'Oh, Rory,' she said, 'it's badly hurt, poor creature. I don't think it will live! I wonder who it belongs to.'

Nobody knew who the dog belonged to. It hadn't a collar on, and the police said that no dog had been reported to them as lost. Rory looked after it all the next day which was Saturday, and tried to make it eat. But it wouldn't.

'Do you think we'd better ask Tammylan to make it better?' said Rory at last. He could no longer bear the pain in the poor dog's eyes.

'I'll fetch him,' said Benjy. Off he sped, and came to Tammylan's cave in about half an hour. He poured out the tale of the dog, and Tammylan nodded his head and said yes, he would come with him.

But when the two of them arrived at the farmhouse, they found Rory almost in tears, big boy though he was. The dog was in his arms, breathing heavily. Its eyes were looking glazed and its paws were limp.

'It's dying,' said Rory, in a trembling voice. 'I can't bear it, Tammylan. I did everything I could. I do like it so much, and it looked at me so gratefully.'

'Don't fret so, Rory,' said Tammylan, putting a gentle hand on the dog's head. 'This dog would never be any use to itself or to others if it lived. Its back is hurt too badly. But it has had a long life and a healthy one. It is an old dog. It would have died in a year or two, anyhow. It must be happy to die in the arms of someone who loves it.'

The dog gave a heavy sigh and then stopped breathing. 'Poor thing,' said Tammylan. 'It is at rest now—no more pain. You could not wish it to live if it could no longer run or hunt, Rory. Give it a good funeral, and put up a little post of wood with its name on.'

'I don't know its name,' said Rory. 'We'll have to put "Here lies a poor dog without a name." '

Everyone was sad because the dog had died. 'I shan't ever want a dog again,' said Rory sadly. 'Not ever. It's spoilt me for having a dog. I only had that dog for a day or two, but it seemed as if I'd loved it for years.'

About a week after that Tammylan came again to the farm. 'Where's Rory?' he asked Sheila, who was busy with the hens.

'Oh, hallo, Tammylan,' said Sheila, looking out of the hen-house at the wild man. 'Rory's in the barn. He's gone all mopey this week, poor Rory—since the dog died, you know.'

Tammylan went swiftly to the barn. He peeped inside. Rory was getting seeds out of a bin. He had lost his usual cheerful expression. He was a boy who, when he felt things, felt them very deeply.

Tammylan went up to Rory. 'I've brought you a present, Rory,' he said. 'Hold out your arms.'

And into Rory's arms he put a fat, round, wriggling little puppy! Rory looked down at it in surprise. His arms tightened over the tiny creature in pleasure.

'Oh, Tammylan—but I don't want a dog now,' he said. 'I don't really. I couldn't love it. This is sweet, but I just don't want it.'

'Well—if you feel like that, of course, you don't need to have it,' said Tammylan, at once. 'But would you mind looking after it for me, just for a day or two, Rory? Then I can take it back to the man who let me have it.'

'Yes—of course I'll mind it for a day or two,' said Rory. 'What sort of dog will it grow into?'

'A collie-dog—like Rascal,' said Tammylan. 'A clever sheep-dog. He'll be a fine fellow.'

Tammylan left the puppy with Rory. Rory ran to show it to the others. Penny squeaked over it in delight, and the puppy frisked round Dopey and the lambs in a most comical way.

'Oh, where did you get it from?' cried Penny. 'Oh, Rory, it's the darlingest puppy I ever saw. What shall we call it? Don't you think Dumpy would be a good name? It *is* such a dumpling.'

'Well—Tammylan brought it to give to me for my own,' said Rory, 'but I said I didn't want another dog— I'd just mind this one for a day or two for him. So we'd better not name it. Anyway Dumpy's a silly name for a dog that's going to grow into a collie! Fancy calling a collie *Dumpy*!'

Rory took the puppy to bed with him that night. It was supposed to sleep in a small cat-basket on the floor—but although it began the night there, it ended it curled up on Rory's toes, a warm little weight. It awoke Rory by licking him on the nose.

It was such a playful little thing. It capered about, and gambolled like a lamb. It had the most ridiculous little bark in the world. It found one of Rory's slippers under the bed and dragged it out in delight. Then it grew tired, curled itself up inside the slipper and went to sleep.

'I'll look after it for you today, if you like,' said Penny. But Rory didn't want anyone else to do that. He took the puppy with him wherever he went. Davey the shepherd saw it and he approved of it.

'That's a fine pup of yours,' he said. 'I can tell he'll be clever. He's got a look of my Rascal about him. You are lucky to have him, Rory.'

'Well,' said Rory, 'I'm not keeping him, you know. I'm just minding him for Tammylan for a day or two.'

The puppy slept on Rory's toes again that night, and once or twice when the boy awoke he stretched out his hand to the pup and patted him. A sleepy pink tongue licked him. There was no doubt about it—the puppy was fine company.

'Rory, if you're not going to keep the puppy, couldn't *I* have him instead?' begged Penny. 'I do love him so. And he would be company for Dopey, Hoppitty and Jumpity. Do let me have him.'

'No,' said Rory, picking up the pup and fondling him. 'He wouldn't love you. He only loves me. He would follow me about all over the place, and then you wouldn't like that.'

The next day Tammylan came to fetch the puppy. He found him capering about Rory's heels as the boy groomed Darling. Rory was talking to him.

'That's right—you bite my heels off! Yes, now go and nibble Darling's great hoof! *She* won't hurt you! Oh, you monkey, you've pulled my shoe-lace undone again!'

'Hello, Rory,' said Tammylan. 'Thanks so much for looking after the little pup for me. I hope he wasn't any bother.'

Rory looked round at Tammylan. He went rather red. 'No bother at all,' he said. 'He's—he's perfect!'

'Yes, he is,' agreed the wild man, looking down at the fat little puppy who was now careering round Tammylan's feet. 'Well—come on, little fellow! Back you go again!' He picked up the puppy. 'Want to say good-bye to him, Rory?' he asked.

'No,' said the boy, in a funny sort of voice, and went on brushing Darling, his back to Tammylan.

'Right,' said the wild man, and went out of the stable, talking to the pup, who was struggling wildly to get out of his arms and go to Rory. 'Now, now, you rascal— you'll have to forget Rory, and come with me. You must have a new little master, who will love you very much.'

Suddenly Rory threw down his brush and ran after Tammylan. 'Tammylan! Don't take him! *I* love him. He's mine, you know he's mine. He wants me for his master. Give him to me!'

'Well, well, now, how you do change your mind!' said the wild man, giving the puppy back to the boy at once. 'Of course you shall have him—didn't I bring him for you? Didn't I choose the best pup out of the litter especially for you?'

Rory took the puppy and squeezed him till the little creature yelped. 'I was silly,' he said. 'I want him awfully. I feel he's just *meant* to be my dog. Oh, Tammylan, I simply couldn't bear it when you said he must forget me and have a new master. I don't want him to forget me.'

'He never will,' said Tammylan gently. 'He knows he is your dog and no one else's. You must feed him and train him and love him, and he will be your constant

103

companion and friend till you grow to be a man, and have a farm of your own.'

'Yes,' said Rory. 'He'll be a true friend to me, I know. And I shall be a true friend to him. Oh, Tammylan—don't you think that would be a wonderful name for him—True? It would be quite good to call, True! True! True! It sounds all right, doesn't it?'

'Quite all right,' said Tammylan, smiling. 'Well—as you won't let me have the pup back, I'll go. Oh, I'll just go and see Penny and her three pets first. Has the kid been eating anything else it shouldn't?'

'Gracious, yes,' said Rory, looking very happy again now. 'I should just think so! It ate Daddy's newspaper yesterday, and we *couldn't* think where it had gone till we saw a bit sticking out of the corner of Dopey's mouth. And it ate my rubber too—my best one. I was cross about that. I just dropped it on the floor, and before I could pick it up, Dopey had eaten it. What it will be like when it's a goat I can't think. It will be a walking dust-bin!'

Tammylan went across to where Penny was playing with Dopey, Jumpity and Hoppitty. She had just fed her lambs from the bottles, and Dopey had tried his best to push them away and take the milk himself. She looked up as Tammylan came to her.

'Oh, Tammylan—have you come to fetch that darling little puppy?' she cried.

'Well—Rory won't let me take it,' said Tammylan, with a smile. Penny gave such a squeal that Dopey jumped two feet in the air with fright, and the lambs darted under a near-by cart.

104

'Oh, Tammylan, is Rory going to keep it? Oh, I shall think of a name for it. Rory, let's call the puppy Tubby—or Roundy—or …'

'He's already got a name,' said Rory. 'I've called him True.'

'Oh—I like that,' said Penny. 'Let's come and tell Mother. There she is!'

Mother was pleased about the puppy. She patted the little thing and smiled at Rory.

'Wasn't it a good thing Tammylan asked me to take care of him for a day or two!' said Rory. Mother laughed. 'Oh—I expect he knew that if he left the pup with you for even a short while, you wouldn't be able to part with it!' she said. 'Tammylan did that on purpose!'

'*Well*!' said Rory, with a delighted chuckle. 'I'll pull old Tammylan's nose for that. Just see if I don't.'

A Little About Dopey and True

Everyone was pleased about the puppy-dog, True. The farmer said he would grow into a fine collie-dog, who would be useful with the sheep.

'But, Daddy, I want him for my companion, not to be with Davey all the time,' said Rory, in dismay.

'Well, my boy, you plan to have a farm of your own when you are grown up,' said his father, 'and maybe you'll keep sheep, just as I do, and will want a good sheep-dog. You could let Davey train True for you whilst he's young, and sometimes help Rascal and the others. Then you will find him of great use to you on your farm, *as* well as a companion.'

'Oh yes—I hadn't thought of that,' said Rory, pleased at the idea of True guarding his sheep for him one day in the future. 'Do you hear that, True? You're going to get a good training. *Two* trainings. One from me to make you into a good farm-dog and companion—and one from Davey and Rascal to make you into a good sheep-dog. Aren't you lucky?'

'Wuff!' answered True, capering round Rory's feet as if he was quite as mad as Dopey the kid. He was so small and fat that it seemed impossible he would ever grow up into a long, graceful collie-dog.

Penny wished he would stay a puppy. It always seemed to her such a pity that young animals grew up in a few months. It took children years to grow up. Animals were quite different.

True was a great success. Even Harriet, who would not put up with any creatures in her kitchen except her cat, Mr By-Himself, liked True running in and out. Mr By-Himself didn't like it at all, however, and made such alarming noises when the puppy dashed into the kitchen, that True set back his ears in fright.

Dopey loved True. Rory said that Dopey had a very bad influence on the puppy. 'The pup is quite mad enough as it is without having Dopey for a friend,' he said. 'Honestly, Penny, I've never seen any creature quite so silly as Dopey.'

Dopey certainly was completely mad. When he was tired of playing with the two lambs, he would caper off by himself, making ridiculous little leaps into the air. He would go into the kitchen and eat the cushion in Harriet's chair. Then when she shooed him out he would go into the dairy and see if he could find a pan of cream to lick. He was able to leap up on to any table with the greatest ease.

Once he even went upstairs into Rory's room and ate all his homework, which Rory had put on the low window-shelf.

Rory was very angry about this and scolded Dopey after he had tried to rescue half a page of French verbs from the kid's mouth. The kid bleated and Penny came running upstairs in fright, wondering what was the matter. She heard Rory scold Dopey and flew into a temper with him.

'Rory! How can you scold a little creature like Dopey? Oh, I do think you're mean.'

'Look here, Penny—I spent a whole hour over my French today,' said Rory, exasperated. 'And that kid of yours has eaten all the pages I wrote. He deserves a much bigger scolding than I've given him. And he'll get some too, if you don't stop him doing this kind of thing.'

'You're horrid,' said Penny, with tears in her eyes. 'As if he could help it! He doesn't know what he's doing. He's only a baby.'

'Penny! He'll go round eating the house down if you don't train him,' said Rory. 'Go away. You're both silly.'

Penny went downstairs, crying. Rory felt rather ashamed of himself, after a time. But he still thought Dopey should be punished. He looked round for the puppy-dog, True. But True was not there.

He went downstairs to look for him. His mother was in the dairy, wrapping up the butter with Sheila.

'Rory! Why have you made Penny cry?' said his mother. 'It's not like you to be unkind.'

'Mother, I *wasn't* unkind,' said Rory. 'It's that tiresome kid of hers. It will keep doing things it shouldn't, so I punished it. That's all. Penny should make it behave better.'

Suddenly there came a wail from the sitting-room, and Rory's mother looked up in dismay. 'Rory! That's Penny. She sounds as if she's hurt herself.'

Rory and Sheila rushed into the sitting-room at once. Penny's wails were so dreadful that both of them

108

thought she must have burnt herself or something. The little girl was holding up her knitting. The needles were out, and all the stitches were coming loose. True, the puppy, was sitting near by, a strand of wool sticking out of his mouth.

Penny looked at him, wailing. She stamped her foot at him. 'You horrid puppy! I don't like you any more! You've spoilt my knitting. Come here!'

Before Rory could stop her she had got hold of True and given him a shake. The puppy fled away, his tail between his legs.

'Penny! How dare you scold True!' cried Rory.

'Well, he's spoilt my knitting. He's a bad dog, and you ought to train him better!' sobbed Penny.

Mother appeared at the door. She burst out into such hearty laughter that the three children stared at her in amazement.

'Mother! What's the joke?' asked Rory, rather indignantly. '*I* don't think it's funny that True should be scolded when he really didn't mean to do harm.'

'And *I* don't think it's funny that my knitting should all be spoilt. It was a scarf for you, Mother,' wept Penny.

'My dear, stupid darlings, I'm not laughing at either of those things,' said Mother, with a chuckle. 'I'm laughing at *you*. First Dopey spoils your homework, Rory, and you scold him and make Penny angry. Then True spoils Penny's knitting, and *she* scolds him, and makes *you* angry. You're quits, aren't you? You have both got naughty little creatures to train, and you must both make allowances for them. Stop crying, Penny. I can easily pick up your stitches for you. And Rory need not do his homework again. I'll write a note to explain things.'

Rory and Penny looked rather ashamed of themselves. 'Thank you, Mother,' said Penny, and ran out of the room with a red face.

'You're right, Mother—we deserve to be laughed at,' said Rory. 'It's very funny. I see that now.'

'Well, what annoyed each of you was that you punished the animal belonging to the other,' said Mother. Make an arrangement between you that if your pets do wrong, no one shall punish them but yourselves. Then things will be quite all right.'

'Mother, you're so sensible,' said Rory, and gave her a hug. 'I love True and I did hate to see Penny scolding him, though I knew I would have punished him myself if I'd discovered what he was doing. And I expect Penny felt the same when I scolded Dopey. I'll go and find Penny.'

'Mother, you're the wisest person in the world!' said Sheila, as they went back to the dairy. She looked out of the window and saw Rory running after Penny. The little girl had her kid in her arms. Rory had True in his.

'Sorry, Penny darling,' said Rory, putting his arm round his little sister and squeezing her. 'Mother says we'd better each punish our own pets, and I think she's right. So if True annoys you, tell me and *I'll* scold him. And if Dopey gets into trouble with me, I'll tell you and *you* shall punish him. See?'

'Yes, Rory,' said Penny, smiling at her big brother through her half-dried tears. 'I do love True, you know that. Do you think he'll hate me for scolding him?'

True licked Penny's nose. Dopey nibbled Rory's sleeve. Both children laughed. 'They've made it up with us,' said Penny happily. 'They don't like quarrelling with us any more than we like it!'

So after that it was an understood thing that pets should only be punished by their owners. True soon learnt what things were considered bad and what things were good, and became a very adorable little puppy, answering eagerly to his name, or to Rory's loud whistle. He lay curled up on Rory's bed at night, and the boy loved him with all his heart. The puppy adored Rory and was always on the look-out for him when he came home from school. Harriet said she was sure he could tell the time from the big kitchen-clock!

'That puppy-dog comes into the kitchen regular as clockwork at just a quarter-to-one,' she said. 'And why does he come there? Because he knows my clock is the only one in this house that's kept exactly right! He's a cunning fellow, he is!'

Benjy loved the puppy very much, but he was careful not to pet him a great deal. All animals preferred Benjy to any of the other children, and sometimes True begged to be allowed to go with Benjy when he was going for a walk. But Benjy knew that Rory wanted him all for his very own, and he would shake his head.

'No, True!' he would say. 'I'm taking Scamper. You wait till Rory can take you. Go and find him!'

Dopey the kid never learnt the difference between right and wrong, no matter how hard Penny tried to teach him. She tried scolding him, reasoning with him,

111

punishing him. He simply did not remember a single thing he was told, and he did the maddest, most stupid things that could be imagined.

'You'll be quite mad when you're a grown-up goat, Dopey, I'm afraid,' Penny would say sadly to him. And she was right. Little Dopey grew from a silly, mad little kid into a silly mad big goat, and though everyone loved him and laughed at him, he did get into more trouble than all the other animals on the farm put together. He just couldn't help it. His appetite was his biggest trouble. He ate everything and anything, from small nails to big posts.

'One day he'll start eating his own tail and he won't be able to stop himself till he's eaten up to his head,' said Benjy solemnly. 'Then that will be the end of poor old Dopey!'

Mark Makes a Lot of Trouble

Mark loved coming to Willow Farm to spend the day and all the children liked him, because, although he knew very little really about farm-life, he was so willing to learn that it was a pleasure to teach him.

He came about once a fortnight, and then he nearly stopped coming because Harriet scolded him for letting the big sow out of the pigsty. Mark hadn't meant to. He stood on the gate and jiggled it, and it suddenly swung open. It was a nice feeling to stand on it whilst it swung back, and Mark began to swing on the gate, to and fro, to and fro.

In the middle of this, the sow, astonished at the sight of the gate opening and shutting so regularly, had the idea that it would be good fun to walk out. So she walked out, her great, fat, round body hardly able to squeeze out between the posts!

'Hey! Don't do that!' shouted Mark, in a panic, and he tried to shut the gate hurriedly. But the sow took no notice of that. She just went on walking, and her great body forced the gate wide open.

It was quite impossible for Mark to make her go back, and he was really rather afraid of her. He ran round her in circles, begging her to return to her sty.

She walked on with her nose in the air, taking not the slightest notice of the anxious boy.

Mark felt most uncomfortable about it. What should he do? Go and tell someone? No—he'd wait till somebody came by. After all, the sow couldn't come to any harm, just taking a walk round the farm.

The sow certainly did not come to any harm—but Harriet's washing did! The sow walked straight into the end-post of the washing-line, and broke it clean in half with her great weight. Down went the clean washing into the dirt!

Out came Harriet, and scolded the sow soundly, picking up her washing as she talked. Then she turned on Mark. 'What did you let that sow out for? You know she mustn't stir from her sty unless Jim takes her. You're a bad boy to make trouble like that, and I've a good mind to tell the farmer. You take that sow back at once.'

'She won't come,' said poor Mark.

'Ho! Won't she!' said Harriet, and picked up a stick. The sow got threatened and she turned round promptly, made for her sty and got herself inside in half a minute! Mark shut the gate tight.

'Now, don't you do a thing like that again,' scolded Harriet. Mark was very red. He hated being scolded, and did not take it in good part as the farm-children did. He almost made up his mind not to come again. But when the children asked him to join them in a picnic the next Sunday, to go and visit Tammylan, he felt he really must go. He wouldn't need to see Harriet!

So at twelve o'clock he was at the farm, ready to set off. Penny popped her head out of the window and called to him.

'We're not quite ready, Mark. Would you mind doing something for me? Would you go to the field where the horses are, and see if the lambs are there? Harriet's going to feed them for me today.'

'Right,' said Mark, and set off to the field. He knew it well. It was a pleasant field, almost a water-meadow, with streams running on three sides, where the horses loved to go and water. He opened the gate, and looked into the field.

'There they are—and Dopey too,' said Mark. He called them in the same high voice that Penny always used to call her pets. 'Come along, come along, come along!'

The three little creatures heard his voice and tore at top speed towards him. They shot out of the gate, capering and gambolling, and Dopey did his best to butt him with his hard little head.

'You rascal!' said Mark, and tried to catch Dopey. But the kid leapt away from him, his tail wriggling and jumped right over Hoppitty. They rushed off to the kitchen, where they could hear Harriet clinking a pail.

Mark followed, laughing. He didn't know that he had forgotten to shut the gate. He had always been told very solemnly and earnestly that every gate must always be shut, and the lesson with the sow should have taught him the importance of this on a farm. But Mark was not so responsible as the other children, and he didn't even think of the open gate, once he had left the field.

Nobody knew that the gate had been left open. It was Sunday, and except for the ordinary everyday work of the farm, such as milking the cows, and feeding the animals and poultry, nothing else was done. The horses had a rest too, and how they enjoyed the quietness and peace of a day in the fields!

The children set off for their picnic, chattering to one another at the tops of their voices. True went with them, and Scamper. Penny badly wanted to take Dopey, but nobody would let her.

'He'll eat all our lunch,' said Rory.

'He'd be under our feet the whole way,' said Sheila.

'He'd do something silly and mad,' said Benjy. So Dopey was left behind with the lambs, bleating in anger, and trying to eat the padlock on the gate that shut him into the orchard.

Tammylan was in his cave, waiting for them all. Mark loved the wild man. He was so kind and wise, he could tell such marvellous tales of animals and birds, he made the children laugh so much, and often he had some wild animal to show them.

Today he took them to a sun-warmed, wind-sheltered copse, where primroses were flowering by the thousand. They shone pale and beautiful in their rosettes of green, crinkled leaves, and on the tiny breeze came their faint, sweet scent.

The children sat down among the primroses and undid their lunch packets. Scamper darted up a near-by tree and leapt from branch to branch. Mark picked a primrose leaf and looked at it.

'I wonder why primrose leaves are always so crinkled,' he said.

'So that the rain may trickle down the crinkles and fall to the outside of the plant, not down into the centre, where the flower-buds are,' said Tammylan.

Mark looked with a new interest at the curious wrinkled leaves. That was the best of Tammylan. He always knew the reasons for everything, and that made the whole out-of-door world so interesting. He knew why sparrows hopped and pigeons walked. He knew why cats could draw back their claws and dogs couldn't.

'Have you any animal to show us today, Tarmmylan?' asked Penny. Tammylan nodded.

'You wait a moment and you'll see him,' he said. The children ate their lunch and waited. In a little while they heard a scrabbling noise in the hedge near by and saw a big prickly brown hedgehog hurrying towards them, his bright little eyes hunting for the wild man.

'Here he is,' said Tammylan, and reached out his hand to the hedgehog. The prickly creature touched it with his nose, then ran all round the wild man, as if to make sure there was every bit of him there!

'Tammylan! Do you remember once you gave me a baby hedgehog for a pet?' said Penny eagerly. 'It went away into the countryside when it grew big. Do you possibly think this could be my hedgehog grown up?'

'It might be, little Penny!' said Tammylan, with a laugh. 'Call it and see!'

117

'Prickles, Prickles!' called Penny, in excitement. To her intense delight the hedgehog, which had curled itself up by the wild man, uncurled itself and looked at Penny inquiringly. She felt perfectly certain that it was her old hedgehog.

'Oh, Prickles, I do hope it's really you,' said the little girl. 'Do you remember how I squirted milk into your mouth with a fountain-pen filler?'

The hedgehog curled itself up again and made no reply. After a moment it gave a tiny little snore.

'I do love the way hedgehogs snore,' said Penny. 'I do really think it's the funniest sound.'

It was fun to be with Tammylan. The rabbits always came out of their holes and sat around when Tammylan was with them. Birds came much nearer. A bog moor-hen came stalking by, and said 'Krek, krek,' politely to the wild man.

'Don't they jerk their heads funnily to and fro?' said Benjy, watching the bird slip into a near-by stream and swim away, its head bobbing like clock-work. 'Oh, Tammylan, what a lot of things people miss if they don't know the countryside well!'

'Yes,' said the wild man dreamily. 'They miss the sound of the wind in the grasses—the way a cloud sails over a hill—the sight of bright brown eyes peering from a hedgerow—the call of an otter at night—the faint scent of the first wild rose …'

The children listened. They liked to hear the wild man talking like this. 'It isn't poetry, but it's awfully like it,' thought Benjy to himself.

It was just at this moment that Mark remembered, with a terrible shock, that he hadn't shut the gate of the horses' field! What made him think of it he couldn't imagine, but he did. The thought slid into his mind. 'I didn't shut that gate when I fetched the lambs! I know I didn't.'

He sat bolt upright, his face scarlet. Tammylan looked at him in surprise.

'What's the matter?' he asked.

'I've just remembered something perfectly awful,' said Mark, in rather a loud voice. Everyone stared at him. 'I—I didn't shut the gate of the horses' field when I went to get Dopey and the lambs,' said Mark. 'Do you suppose the horses are all right?'

'You *are* an idiot, Mark,' said Rory, sitting up too. 'How many times have you got to be told to shut gates, before you remember it? All the horses may have got out and be wandering goodness knows where!'

'Wouldn't someone see the gate was open and shut it?' said Mark hopefully.

'No. It's Sunday,' said Benjy. 'Look here—we'd better get back and see if the horses are all right. We can't have them wandering half over the country. Daddy wants them for work tomorrow.'

The picnic was broken up at once. The wild man was sorry, but he said of course the children must go back and see. 'And you had better *all* go,' he said, 'because if the horses have wandered away, you'll want everyone giving a hand in the search. Come again another day.'

The children set off home. They said no more to Mark about the open gate, and did not grumble at him—but he felt most uncomfortable because by his silly carelessness he had spoilt a lovely picnic.

Their father and mother saw them trooping down over Willow Hill, above the farm, and were most astonished.

'You've soon finished your picnic!' cried their mother. 'Why are you home so early? It isn't nearly tea-time.'

'I left the gate of the horses' field open,' said Mark. 'We've come to see if the horses are still there all right. I'm most terribly sorry.'

The children ran to the big field where the horses lived. They saw Darling near by. Then Rory saw Captain and Blossom drinking from the stream. Good—the three cart-horses were safe.

But where were Patchy and Ebony, the two new horses? The children slipped into the field, and shut the gate behind them.

They looked carefully all round the big field—but there was no doubt about it, the two new horses had gone.

'The shire-horses would be too sensible to wander off, even if they saw the gate was open,' said Rory. 'Oh dear—where can the other two have got to?'

They went to tell their father. He looked grave. 'I'd better get the car out and see if I can see them anywhere down the lanes,' he said. 'You children scout about a bit and see if you can find out if anyone has seen stray horses.'

Then began such a hunt. The five children separated and searched all over the farm to find the missing horses. It was a serious thing to lose horses, because, although they were certain to be found again some time or other, some days might pass before they were traced—and that meant so many hours' work on a farm left undone for lack of the horses to do it. Loss of labour was loss of money on a farm.

Mark hunted harder than anyone, for he felt guilty and was ready to search till he dropped, if only he could find the missing horses in the end. Suddenly he gave a loud shout and pointed to something on the ground. The others came up, one at a time, panting to see what he had found.

'Look—hoof-marks! That's the way they went,' said Mark excitedly, pointing away from the farm, up Willow Hill. 'We must follow these prints until we find the horses. Come on!'

Where Can the Horses Have Gone?

The children ran to tell their parents that they had found hoof-marks and were going to track them. 'We'll bring back Patchy and Ebony, *you'll* see!' said Benjy. 'Even if we have to follow them for miles.'

'You may quite well have to,' said the farmer. 'I can't come with you, because I've got a man coming to see me about a new bull. I'll go hunting in the car after that.'

'Penny's not to go,' said the children's mother firmly. 'I'm not going to let her rush for miles. She's too little.'

'*Mother*! I'm *not* little any more!' cried Penny indignantly. 'It isn't fair. When you want me to do anything you tell me I'm a great big girl, big enough to do what you want. And when you don't want me to do anything, you say I'm too little. Which am I, little or big?'

'Both!' said her mother, with a laugh. 'A dear little girl who does what she's told—and a great big girl who never makes a fuss about it!'

Everyone laughed—even Penny. 'Mother's too clever for you, Penny,' said Rory. 'Stay behind and look after True for me, will you, there's a dear. I can't take him with me.'

The idea of looking after True was so nice that Penny at once gave up the pleasure of going to hunt for lost horses. She held out her arms eagerly for the fat little pup. He snuggled up to her and she took him indoors to play with.

The others set off up the hill after the hoof-marks. They could see them easily. They followed them right to the top of the hill and then down to the east.

Rory stood on the top of the hill, shaded his eyes and looked down into the next valley, and over the common that lay to the east.

'I can't see a sign of the horses,' he said. 'Not a sign.'

'Well, come on, we've got the hoof-marks to guide us,' said Benjy, and the four set off down the hill.

They followed the marks for two or three miles. It was tiring. The prints went on and on, often very difficult to see. Sometimes the children lost them for a while and then found them again after a ten-minute hunt to the right and left.

'Bother these horses!' said Rory. 'Why couldn't they have stayed somewhere near instead of taking a ten-mile walk!'

'Surely we'll come up to them soon,' said Mark.

They went on. After another hour they came to the common—and here, alas, the hoof-marks disappeared entirely. Not a sign of them was to be seen. The children stared hopelessly over the wide expanse of common.

'It's no good hunting over the common,' said Benjy. 'We might hunt all day and night and never see the horses. We'd better go back.'

'I'm so hungry,' said Rory. 'It's long past tea-time. Come on.'

The four children were disappointed, hungry and miserable, especially Mark. He didn't say a single word all the way home. Sheila was sorry for him and walked beside him. She guessed how he was feeling.

When they got back Penny rushed out to meet them. 'Have you got the horses? Where were they?'

Rory shook his head. 'The hoof-marks led to the common, Penny—and there we had to stop and turn back—because there were no more marks to follow. We couldn't hunt the common. It's too big.'

'Poor children,' said Mother, coming out too. 'Go and wash. I've a lovely Sunday tea for you. Hurry now.'

They couldn't hurry, even for a lovely tea, hungry though they were! But they felt much better after eating slices of ham, new-boiled eggs, hot scones and butter, and one of Harriet's currant cakes. True darted under the table, pulling everyone's laces undone. There was no stopping him doing that! He seemed to think that shoe-laces were tied up merely for him to pull undone.

After a while the farmer came in and sat down to a late tea too. He had been scouring the countryside in his car, looking far and wide for the horses. He had notified the police of their loss and was hoping that at any moment he might hear where they were and go and fetch them.

But nothing was heard of the horses that evening and Mark felt so dreadful that he was near to bursting into tears.

'It looks as if we'll have to let one of the cart-horses do the milk-round tomorrow morning,' said the farmer, 'That's a nuisance, because I wanted him in the fields. Such a waste of time!'

'I'm very sorry, sir, for leaving the gate open,' said Mark, stammering over his words, and feeling rather frightened of the worried farmer.

'I bet you won't do it again,' said Rory.

'Leaving a gate open is a very small thing,' said the farmer, 'but unfortunately small things have a way of leading to bigger things. An open gate—wandering cattle or horses—maybe damage done by them to be paid for—loss of hours of their labour—loss of our time looking for them. It all means a pretty big bill when you add it up. But we all make mistakes, Mark—and providing we learn our lessons and don't make the same mistakes twice, we shan't do so badly. Don't worry too much about it. You can't afford to be careless on a farm. Those horses will turn up sooner or later, so cheer up!'

Mark went home, not at all cheerful. The others went to bed, tired out. Rory was asleep almost before True had settled down on his feet.

In the morning there was still no sign of the missing horses, and Darling had to be harnessed to the milk-cart for the milk-round. Jim grumbled at this because he wanted her for heavy field-work. Blossom was put to the farm-wagon to take root-crops to the field where the sheep were grazing. This was usually work one of the light horses did. The children went off to school.

125

Fanny and Harriet were just as upset about the missing horses as everyone else. 'I wish I could find those horses,' Fanny said, a dozen times that morning.

And then, when she went into the yard to fetch a broom, she heard a faint sound that made her turn her head.

'That's a horse's whinny, sure as I'm standing here!' said the girl, and she listened again. She heard the noise once more, borne on the wind. It seemed to come from the next farm, whose fields adjoined Willow Farm. She rushed in to Harriet.

'Aunt Harriet! I believe those horses are in Marlow's Field!' she cried. 'I heard them whinnying, and Farmer Marlow hasn't any horses in his field, has he?'

'Not that I know of,' said Harriet. 'Well—you'd better go and look, that's all. You can sweep out the kitchen when you come back.'

Fanny sped off to the next farm. She went across one of the Willow Farm fields, splashed through a stream for a short cut, and then made her way into the field belonging to Farmer Marlow. He only had a small farm, and went in for crops, not livestock.

The girl looked about the big field she had come into—and, to her enormous delight, she saw Patchy and Ebony standing at the far end! To think they had been there, all the time, within five minutes' walk, and not miles and miles away!

The girl called to them. 'Patchy! Come here! Ebony, come along. Come along!'

Where Can the Horses Have Gone?

The horses cantered over to her. They knew her for one of the people belonging to Willow Farm. She took hold of their manes and pulled them gently.

'Bad creatures! You've had everyone worrying about you and hunting for you for hours! Now you come along with me, and don't you wander away again, even if our gate *is* left open!'

The horses came along willingly enough. They had wandered out of the open gate and had made their way slowly to Farmer Marlow's deserted field. No one had noticed them there at all. They had not had the sense to find their way back again, but had stayed there together all the night, waiting for someone to find them.

Fanny proudly marched them back to the farmhouse. To think of everyone hunting away for them—and she, Fanny, had found them! Her aunt, the cook, heard the clip-clop of the hoofs in the farmyard outside, and came out.

'Good girl!' she said. 'Well, well—I'm right glad they're back again. They look a bit ashamed of themselves, don't they? You give a call to Jim and tell him you've got them. Then come back and sweep out the kitchen.'

Fanny went off with the horses and shouted to Jim. He was amazed when he turned round and saw Fanny with the horses.

'Where did they come from?' he asked, staring.

Oh, I got them from Farmer Marlow's field,' said Fanny, feeling quite a heroine. 'They must have been there all the time, and nobody noticed them.'

Jim took Patchy and Ebony, and soon they were at their work, happy to be back again with the others. They whinnied to the big cart-horses, and seemed to be telling them all that had happened.

That morning, when he got to school, Mark asked Rory anxiously about the horses, and was very upset when he heard that they had not yet returned. All the children were gloomy, and they did not expect for one moment that Patchy and Ebony would have been found by the time they returned on their donkeys to their dinner.

But what a surprise for them! When they got near to Willow Farm, Rory gave a shout.

'I say! There's old Patchy—look! And there's Ebony—see, in that wagon with Bill. Hey, Bill! Hey! Where did the horses turn up from after all?'

'You ask Fanny,' said Bill, with a grin. 'She's the clever one!'

So Fanny had the delight of telling and re-telling her little story to four admiring children. They crowded round her, listening. It was a great moment for the girl.

'Well, to think of us following those hoof-marks all those miles!' said Rory, with a groan. 'Miles and miles! What idiots we were!'

'They must have been old marks,' said Benjy. 'Now, if only Tammylan had been here, he would have told us at once that those marks had been made ages ago, and we'd have known they were no good to follow. I say—won't old Mark be pleased?'

He was! His round, red face was one beam of joy when the children told him, at afternoon school, how the horses had been found.

'They were just four or five minutes' walk away from us all the time we were at the farm, and we never knew it,' said Rory.

'I shall never be careless again,' said Mark. 'That *has* taught me a lesson.'

It certainly had. Poor Mark got into such a habit of shutting gates and doors behind him that he couldn't leave them open when he was told to! 'I think all this ought to be put into a book, to warn other children,' he said solemnly to his mother.

'Maybe one day it will,' she answered.

And so it has.

Willow Farm Grows Larger!

The Easter holidays came and went. The summer term began, and the children galloped their donkeys across the fields to school. It was lovely to canter over the emerald green meadows, and to see the trees putting out green fingers everywhere.

Penny liked the beech leaves best. She had discovered that each leaf inside its pointed bud was pleated just like a tiny fan, and she had been amazed and delighted.

'Who pleats them?' she asked Sheila. But Sheila didn't know.

'I suppose they just grow like that,' she said.

Yes, but *some*body must have pleated each leaf into those tiny folds,' said Penny, puzzled. 'I shall ask Tammylan.'

Penny was very busy before and after school hours with Dopey and the lambs. She fed them and played with them and they followed her around as if they were dogs. They had all grown very fast indeed, and looked strong and healthy. Davey was delighted with the two lambs. 'My word, Tuppenny, you made a better mother to my lambs than the ewes do themselves!' he said, with a laugh.

'Davey, is that poor mother-sheep all right that got caught in the wire?' said Penny.

'Quite all right,' said Davey. 'I believe she would have had her lambs back again in a week's time—but I hadn't the heart to take them away from you!'

'I wouldn't have let you!' cried Penny. 'I just *love* Hoppitty and Jumpity. But I wish they weren't getting so big.'

'Oh, it doesn't matter your lambs growing,' said Davey, 'but it's that kid of yours I'm sorry to see getting big! He'll be the wildest goat we ever had on the farm. He came up here yesterday, and bless me if he didn't find my old hat in my hut and chew it to bits.'

'Oh, Davey—I'll give you a new one for your birthday!' cried Penny. 'Isn't Dopey bad? I just can't teach him to be any better. He nearly drives Harriet mad. He *will* jump in through the low kitchen window and chase Mr By-Himself.'

'Ho!' said Davey, with a chuckle, 'that won't do that sulky old cat any harm. I'll give Dopey a good mark for that!'

'Isn't our flock of sheep getting big?' said Penny as she looked down the hillside at the sheep and lambs grazing together. 'Willow Farm is getting larger and larger, Davey. Sheila and Fanny have heaps of young chicks and ducklings again, so we'll soon have hundreds of hens and ducks! And you know we've got lots of new piglets? They are so sweet!'

'Ah, the springtime brings new life everywhere,' said Davey. 'I reckon we'll soon be having little calves, too.'

131

'Oh! Is Daddy going to buy some?' cried Penny, skipping for joy. 'Oh, last year we had some dear little calves and I fed them out of the milk-pail. It was lovely to feel them sucking my fingers, Davey.'

Mark came to spend the day, and Penny ran to show him all the new creatures that had arrived since he had last been to the farm. He was very interested in the piglets.

'Did you buy them?' he asked. 'I do like them.'

'No, the sow bore them,' said Penny. Mark stared at her. 'We didn't buy them. They belong to the old sow.'

Mark didn't understand. Penny thought he was very silly. She wondered how to explain to him about kittens and puppies and calves and lambs and piglets.

'Listen, Mark,' she said. 'You know hens lay eggs, don't you?'

'Yes,' said Mark.

'Well, silly, cats lay kittens, and dogs lay puppies, and pigs lay piglets, and cows lay calves, and hens lay eggs with chicks in them, and ducks lay eggs with ducklings in them and turkeys lay eggs with baby turkeys in, and geese lay eggs with goslings in them, and—and—and—'

'Well, of course!' said Mark, thinking what a silly he had been. 'Of course—how lovely! Let's go and ask Jonquil the cow what she thinks her little calf will be like when it's born.'

They went to the big field where the cows were kept and looked for Jonquil. She was a red and white cow, with big soft eyes, a great favourite with the children.

132

Cows rarely look for caresses, but Jonquil was different from most cows. If the children came near, she would turn her big head and ask for a pat or stroke on her nose.

'Wherever is Jonquil?' wondered Penny. The two children counted the cows. They had sixteen at Willow Farm—but now they could only count fifteen.

'We'd better look for her,' said Penny. 'Come on, Mark.'

They went round the big field, which had many old willow trees here and there—and behind one big hollow tree, its long branches springing high into the air, they found the red and white cow.

She was standing in the tall grass there, looking lovingly down at a little red and white heap on the grass. Penny and Mark ran up to see what it was. Then Penny gave one of her piercing squeals.

'Oh, Oh! It's Jonquil's calf! It's born! Oh, look at the dear, darling little thing! It's *exactly* like Jonquil. Isn't it, Mark? Oh, Jonquil, it's lovely, it's lovely!'

Jonquil gazed at the two children. She was very proud of her little long-legged calf, which had been born only a little while before. She bent her head down and licked it. The calf raised its head and looked at its mother.

'Isn't it sweet?' said Mark. 'I do think baby things are lovely. I wish you'd let me help you to feed the calf, Penny.'

'Well, you can if you come to see it,' promised Penny generously. 'I do, do hope it's a girl-calf. Daddy says the boy-calves have to be sold when they are three weeks old. But we are going to keep the girl-calves this year because they grow up into cows, which give milk and are valuable.'

'Oh,' said Mark, who felt that he was learning a great deal that afternoon. 'I say—why do you have to feed this calf, Penny? Surely its mother can give it all the milk it wants, because she's a cow!'

'Ah, but Daddy says that when a cow has a calf, she has such wonderful rich milk that it's good for children and grown-ups,' said Penny, looking very wise. 'So we take the calf from its mother after a little while, and feed it on separated milk ...'

'Whatever's that?' asked Mark.

'It's the milk that's had the cream taken away, Mark,' said Penny, feeling quite clever as she related all this to the big boy. 'Last year I put a few drops of cod-liver oil into the milk to make up for the cream that wasn't there.'

'I do think you know a lot, Penny,' said Mark, look-ing admiringly at the little girl. She felt pleased. It was so tiresome always to be the youngest and smallest and to have to ask the others things she wanted to know —and here she was, telling a big boy all kinds of things he didn't seem to know at all. It was marvellous. Penny felt quite swollen with importance.

'Let's go and tell Daddy about Jonquil's calf,' said Penny. She took Mark's hand and they went to find the farmer. He was two fields away, hard at work.

'Daddy! Jonquil's got a lovely little new-born calf!' shouted Penny. The farmer looked up at once. 'Where is it?' he asked anxiously.

'Come and see,' said Penny. 'Oh, Daddy, I hope it's a girl-calf, then we can keep it. We had three last year, and they were all girl-calves. I was sorry when you sold them—but we kept them a long time, didn't we?'

The farmer went to see Jonquil's calf. It certainly was a pretty little thing.

'But it's a boy-calf!' he told Penny. 'Yes—a little bull-calf. So you must make up your mind to lose it in three or four weeks' time, Penny.'

Penny looked ready to cry. She had so badly wanted the calf to be a girl. 'Cheer up,' said her father. 'Daisy is having a calf, too—so maybe she will present you with a girl that you can feed for months! Now—what are you going to call this one? He's a fine little fellow.'

Penny cheered up when she had to think of a name. She turned to Mark. 'What shall we call him? Let's think hard.'

'Radish, because he's red,' said Mark.

'Don't be silly,' said Penny. 'Nobody ever heard of a cow called Radish.'

'Well, *I've* never heard of a cow called Jonquil before,' said Mark.

'That's because you haven't known many cows,' said Penny. 'You ought to know that most cows are called by the names of flowers.'

'Well—let's call the calf Peony, then,' said Mark. 'That's red too.'

'It's the wrong red,' said Penny, who didn't really mean to let Mark choose the name himself. 'And

135

besides, this is a boy-calf. Peony sounds like a name for a girl-calf. Let *me* think.'

But before she could think of a good name, the other three children came running up, with Fanny behind them, to see the new calf. It was always such a thrill when any new animal arrived—especially one born on the farm itself. Jonquil stood patiently by whilst everyone admired her new-born.

'It's beautiful, Jonquil,' said Sheila, giving the tiny calf her fingers to suck. 'You ought to call your boy-calf Johnnie, after you, Jonquil!'

'Oh *yes!*' said Penny. 'That's lovely. Jonquil, your calf is christened Johnnie.'

And Johnnie he was, and Johnnie he remained even after he was sold at the market, three or four weeks later. Penny went with her father when he took him to market, and she told the buyer that the calf was called Johnnie.

'So please go on calling him that,' she said. 'He's nice. I've been feeding him out of a pail, and he's really very good.'

'I'll look after Johnnie, Missy,' said the man, with a smile.

Daisy had her calf not long afterwards, and to Penny's joy it was a girl-calf, so it was allowed to live on at the farm. 'I shall have you for months and months,' said Penny to the soft-eyed little creature, as she and Mark took turns at feeding it, dipping their fingers into the pail of milk and then letting the calf suck. 'Perhaps Daddy might even let you stay with us

136

for always till you grow into a cow. That would be lovely.'

It was fun to be on the farm in the late spring and early summer, when the whole place was full of young new things. And how they grew! The little lambs grew big and no longer frisked quite so madly. The calves grew. The chicks turned into young hens and the ducklings into ducks. The piglets grew as fat as butter. In the hedges new young wild birds were seen, and tiny baby rabbits scampered on the hillside among the sheep.

'It's lovely to see so many things growing up,' said Sheila. 'They're all growing as fast as the corn in the fields—but it's a pity they stop being funny and get solemn and proper.'

There was one little creature that grew too—but he didn't become solemn and proper. No—Dopey remained as funny and as mad as ever. He just simply *couldn't* grow up!

Good Dog True

One of the animals that grew the fastest of all was Rory's puppy, True. For a few weeks he was a round ball of a pup, his short legs hardly seeming able to carry his fat little body.

'Now he's sort of got *longer*,' said Penny, looking at him one day. 'Hasn't he, Rory? He's not so fat. It's a good thing we didn't call him Dumpy.'

Everyone looked at True. He was sitting in his basket, his head on one side, his bright eyes looking at Rory. Rory's heart warmed with love towards him. He thought secretly that never since the world began could there have been such a wonderful puppy as True.

True wagged his tail as he saw the boy's eyes on him. He leapt out of the basket and ran to his master. He put his paws up on his knee.

Yes—he *is* growing,' said Penny. 'His nose is getting longer too—not so snubby. I believe he will be awfully like Rascal. I should think he'll be every bit as clever too.'

'Oh, much cleverer,' said Rory, at once. 'Why, he already walks to heel whenever I tell him, and do you know, yesterday I made him sit on my school satchel and guard it, whilst I walked on for a quarter of a mile!'

*He was sitting in his basket, his head on one side, his
bright eyes looking at Rory.*

'And did he guard it?' asked Penny, with great interest. 'Didn't he run after you and leave it?'

'Of course not!' said Rory scornfully. 'He knows better than that! He just sat on that satchel, looking after me as I went off, and he didn't stir from it till I suddenly turned round and whistled to him!' 'How clever of him!' said Sheila.

'He was even cleverer than that,' said Rory. 'He tried to bring the satchel with him! He pulled and pulled at it with his baby teeth, and in the end everything spilt out of it, and when it was empty it was light enough for him to drag along to me. You should just have seen him, dragging it along, falling over the strap, trying to get to me. I did laugh.'

'Aren't you going to let Davey have a hand in his training soon?' asked Daddy. 'Or rather—let Rascal teach him a few things. After all, he's a sheep-dog, you know, and ought to use his fine, quick brain for good work.'

'Oh, I know, Daddy,' said Rory. 'I'm taking him up to Davey tomorrow. It's Saturday, and I can watch him having his first lesson.'

'I'll come too,' said Penny.

'Well, don't bring Dopey,' said Rory. 'I don't feel very kindly towards him at the moment. He's eaten my best handkerchief.'

'I won't bring him,' promised Penny. So the next day, when Rory yelled to Penny that he was going up the hill to find Davey, Penny hurriedly shut Dopey into a shed, and ran to join Rory and True.

140

Dopey was most annoyed at being shut up. He was mad and silly, but he always had brains enough to try and outwit anyone who wanted to shut him up. He scrambled up on a bin that stood beneath a window. He butted the window with his small, tough head and it opened a little way. He butted it again, bleating at it. It opened wide enough for him to jump out. With a flying leap the kid was out into the yard, startling the hens there enormously. They fled away, clucking.

Dopey ran at them, just for fun. Then he went to say a few rude words to the piglets who lived with their big sow-mother in the sty. Then he looked around for Penny.

The little girl was half-way up the hill with Rory and True. Her clear high voice came floating to Dopey's sharp ears. With bounds, leaps and jumps he was off after her, only pausing to leap at a scared rabbit that shot into its hole in fright.

'Penny! There's Dopey!' said Rory, in disgust. 'I asked you to shut him up.'

'Well, I *did*!' said Penny, in astonishment. 'I put him into the shed. How did he get out?'

Only Dopey knew, and he wasn't going to tell. He frisked round True and tried to bite his tail. Then he butted him with his head. True snapped at him playfully. He liked Dopey and the lambs.

'Catch the kid and shut him up in that little old sheep-hut there,' said Rory. But that was easier said than done! Dopey had brains enough to know that Penny meant to shut him up again, and he skipped out of her way

141

whenever she went near him. He could be most exasperating. Penny gave it up at last.

'Oh well, I dare say it won't make any difference, him being here when True gets his first lesson,' said Rory at last. 'Come on. Hallo, Davey!'

'Good morning, young sir! Good morning, Tuppenny!' said the old shepherd, his eyes wrinkling in the sun as he turned to look at them both. 'You've brought little True for his lesson, I see.'

'Yes,' said Rory proudly. 'He's as clever as can be, Davey. Where's Rascal?'

'Over there, with Nancy and Tinker,' said Davey. He whistled, and the three dogs came running up to him. The shepherd turned to Rory.

'I'll get the dogs to take the sheep down the hill, and then bring them up again,' he said. 'True must run with Rascal. Tell him.'

'True! Rascal!' called Rory. The dogs came up, True wagging his tail so fast that it could hardly be seen. 'Now listen, True. You're to keep with Rascal. See?' said Rory. 'Rascal, see that True is by your side!'

Rascal understood perfectly. He had taught Tinker and Nancy, and he knew that this young pup was to be trained too. He liked the look of him!

Davey gave a few sharp orders to the dogs. He used as few words as possible, and pointed with his stick. Each of the grown dogs knew exactly what he meant. They were, for some reason, to take the sheep down the hill, and then to bring them up again. Rascal nosed True gently to make him start off with them.

The three dogs and the puppy set off together. At first True thought it was just a run, and he enjoyed scurrying along. Then he found that the sheep were running too. Ah—that was even more fun. Were they chasing the sheep? That was really rather strange, thought True, because Rory had already taught him not to chase the hens, ducks or cats.

He made up his mind that they *were* chasing the sheep, and he ran at one, trying to snap at its hind legs. But that was quite the wrong thing to do! Rascal was beside him in a moment, pushing him away, talking to him in dog-language.

'Silly pup! You should never frighten a sheep. We are running them down the hill, that's all, not chasing them. Help to keep them together in a bunch!'

True felt ashamed of himself. His quick mind saw that the dogs were now bunching the sheep together, and taking them somewhere. He must help.

So, when he saw a sheep leaving the flock, he ran to it. He nosed it back again into the flock.

'Good dog True!' shouted Rory proudly. 'Did you see that, Davey? Did you see that, Penny? He's learning already!'

The dogs took the sheep down to the bottom of the hill. Rascal looked back at the shepherd to make quite sure that he still wanted them brought back again. Davey waved his stick. Rascal understood. He *was* to take them up again. The dog was a little puzzled, because there did not seem much sense to him in this order, but he was used to obeying.

143

True was running with him now, trying to do all that Rascal was doing. He ran round the flock to keep them together.

'He's learning to bunch them already!' said Rory. It was more difficult to get the sheep back up the hill again than it had been to run them down. They did not want to go. They wanted to stay there and graze. The three grown dogs did their best to send them up the hill, but it took time. True grew tired of this new game. He ran off by himself and put his nose in a rabbit hole.

'Hey, True! Hey, hey!' yelled Rory. 'Back to your work again at once.'

'Rascal! Fetch True!' ordered Davey. The amazingly wise sheep-dog understood. He ran off at once to the puppy and pushed him smartly back to work again. True was not too pleased, for he felt sure he could go down a hole and get a rabbit just then. But he ran round the sheep once more and they began to move slowly back up the hill, trying to stop and nibble the grass every now and again, but driven steadily onwards by the three dogs and the puppy.

Then Dopey chose that moment to try and behave like a sheep-dog too. He began to run round the sheep and to butt them with his hard little head. But the sheep were not standing any nonsense of that sort from a kid! They didn't mind obeying the dogs, whom they sensed to be their guardians and friends—but to be told what to do by a silly little kid! No—that was too much!

With one accord all the nearby sheep turned on Dopey and ran at him. He found himself enclosed in the flock, and could not get out! He was squeezed by the fat woolly bodies of the sheep. He was lost. He bleated pitifully.

Rory and Davey laughed till the tears came into their eyes. 'It serves him right,' said Rory.

'Oh, poor little Dopey!' said Penny, half laughing too. 'Let me go and rescue him.'

'No, you stay where you are,' said Rory. 'It will do Dopey good to be squashed by the sheep. He thinks far too much of himself! Look—there he is!'

Dopey had managed to get free from the sheep when the dogs moved them on again, and he came leaping out from the flock, looking really scared. He sprang right over True and Rascal and leapt up the hill to Penny faster than he had ever moved before!

'Little silly!' said Penny, picking him up. He was still small enough to be carried, though he wouldn't be much longer. 'Did you think you were a sheep-dog, then?'

The sheep were brought right back to the shepherd and he told the dogs to lie down. They lay down, panting, their watchful eyes turning to their flock every now and again. True lay down with them too, feeling most important.

'He's done some work for the first time in his life, and he's feeling good,' said Davey. 'Well done, little True. We'll make a fine sheep-dog of you yet, so we will. You'll be as good as my Rascal.'

'He'll be better,' said Rory.

Davey laughed. 'Maybe,' he said. 'We'll see. I'd trust Rascal to look after my sheep for me if I had to go away for a week! He can count them more quickly than I can, because if one is missing he knows it sooner than I do, and is off to find it. What I'd do without my dogs I don't know.'

'And I don't know what I'd do without True now,' said Rory, picking up the puppy and fondling his ears. 'Come on, True—back home we go! You shall have an extra good feed as a reward for working hard at your first real lesson!'

So back they went and True certainly did have a good meal. Dopey came to share it with him. The little kid thought he had worked as hard as the puppy, and he didn't see why he shouldn't have a reward too!

The Coming of the Bees

'Mother, don't you want to keep bees?' asked Sheila, one day, as she helped herself to some golden honey out of the pot. 'You said you were going to.'

'So I did,' said Mother. 'Well—I'll talk to the bee-man about them today. I've got to go into the village and I'll really see if we can't get a hive or two and keep bees.'

'Oooh!' said Penny. 'Lovely! I shall like bees. I think they are such happy things.'

'Why happy?' asked Rory in surprise.

'Well, I hum when I'm happy, and bees are always humming, so they must always be very happy,' said Penny. Everyone laughed. Penny did have such funny ideas.

Mother went down to the village to talk to the bee-man. When the children came back from school that day she told them that she had arranged for two hives of bees. Everyone was thrilled.

'Will there be enough nectar in the flowers we've got to keep two hives going?' asked Rory. 'We haven't really got a great many flowers in our garden, have we, Mother? The farm garden mostly grows salads and things like sage and thyme that Harriet uses for seasoning things.'

'Oh, bees love thyme,' said Mother. 'But we have plenty of other near-by flowers growing by the thousand—by the million—that bees love, and can make honey from.'

'What flowers?' asked Penny in surprise.

'Well—what about Daddy's clover field?' said Mother. 'Haven't you walked by that and seen and heard the bees humming there by the hundred? Clover is full of nectar for them. You know that, Penny darling, because I have often seen you pull a clover flower head, and pick out the little white or pink tubes from the head and suck them to taste the sweet nectar inside!'

'Yes, I have,' said Penny, remembering. 'It tastes as sweet as this honey!'

'And then there is the heather on the near-by common,' said Mother. 'When that is in flower, the bees swarm there in their thousands! Heather honey is most delicious. Oh, our bees will be able to fill the combs in their hives with any amount of sweet honey for us!'

'Do they have brushes as well as combs?' asked Penny. Everyone roared with laughter.

'Idiot!' said Rory. 'Mother, you wouldn't possibly think Penny was nine, would you?'

'Don't tease her,' said Mother, looking at the red-faced girl. 'Yes—they do have brushes, funnily enough! You know, they collect pollen from the flowers too, and put it into tiny pockets in their legs. Well, they have brushes on their legs to brush the powder! So they *do* have brushes and combs! But the combs are for holding the honey. I'll show you some empty ones when the hives come.'

One evening the bee-man came. The two white-painted hives had already arrived, and were set up in Mother's own piece of garden, just behind the farm-house. The children were on the look-out for the bee-man. He was a funny little fellow, with a wrinkled face like an old, old apple, and eyes as black as ripe pear-pips. He had a funny high voice that squeaked.

'Good evening to you, Mam,' he said to Mother. 'Now, where are the hives? Ah, we'll have to move them from there, so we will. I'll tell you where to put them.'

'Does it matter where we have them?' asked Mother. 'I rather thought I'd like to have them there on the lawn so that I could see them from my window.'

'We'll put them over the other side,' said the bee-man. 'You can still see them from the window then. You see, Mam, there's a gap in the hedge just behind where you've put the hives, and the wind will blow cold on them when it's in that quarter. Ah, bees don't like a draught. Never did. Over there will be splendid.'

So the hives were moved. Then the bee-man dressed himself up in a most peculiar way. He put on a funny broad-brimmed hat, and then put on some puffed white sleeves. Then he pulled a black veil out of his bag, and put that over his head and tucked it in at his waist.

'What's all that for?' asked Rory. 'Are you afraid of getting stung?'

No,' said the bee-man. 'But I want to be sure that no bee gets up my sleeve, or down my neck, because if one does, it will get squashed and will sting me—not that I mind that overmuch but I don't want to kill any of these bees. A bee will always sting if it's squeezed or squashed!'

Penny was not quite sure if she liked having so many bees close to her. The bee-man had brought them with him, and was going to put them into the hives. Clouds of them flew about, and the children began to move away.

One buzzed round Penny's head and she gave a squeal. Then she turned and ran.

'Now what's the use of running from bees?' said the bee-man scornfully. 'Don't you know they can out-fly even the fastest train! You stand your ground, Missy. They won't sting you if you don't interfere with them.'

'You've got some on your belt,' said Sheila.

The bee-man flicked them away as if they were bits of dust. He didn't mind them at all. Some crawled over his hands and he shook them off.

'Did they sting you?' asked Rory.

'Not they!' said the bee-man. 'Look—you've a couple of bees on your arm, my boy. You flick them away as I do!'

So Rory did and the bees flew off into the air. Mother showed Penny the comb full of holes in which the bees would store their honey. 'They will seal each hole up when it is full,' she said. 'You shall have honey-in-the-comb to eat later on in the season. You will like that.'

The Coming of the Bees

The bees soon settled into the hives. It was fun to see them each day, sailing up into the air, getting their bearings as it were, and then flying straight off to the clover-fields. There was such a coming and going all day long!

'It must be hot in the hives today,' said Sheila, one very hot morning. 'Mother has put an electric fan into the dairy to make it even cooler. I guess the bees wish they could have an electric fan in their hives too.'

'They cool their hives quite well themselves,' said Daddy. 'If you could look inside the hive you would see that many of the bees have been given the job of standing still and whirring their wings to make a cool draught. They are the electric fans of the hive!'

'Well—that's marvellous!' said Penny, only half believing this. But Daddy spoke the truth, and the inside of the hives was kept cool in this way by the bees themselves on very hot days.

Harriet liked the bees. She could hear their humming from the kitchen window, and it was very pleasant. Penny liked sitting on the low kitchen window-sill, listening to the bees outside, whilst she ate a scone hot out of the oven.

'Harriet, did you know that we've got another calf born today?' she said, as she ate. 'It belongs to Pimpernel.'

'There now!' exclaimed Harriet, pleased. 'We shall have some wonderful rich milk from Pimpernel, and be able to make the finest butter you ever saw. Be sure you tell the bees about it, Penny dear.'

151

'Tell the bees?' said Penny in great astonishment. 'Why should I tell the bees?'

'Oh, don't you know you should tell the bees whenever anything happens in a household?' said Harriet, who was full of country customs. 'You should always tell them when there is a death in the household, or any change—and they like to hear of such happenings as a new calf being born. It brings good luck to the household if you tell the bees the news. You go and tell them, Penny.'

Penny went first to tell her mother what Harriet had said. Mother laughed. 'Oh, I don't expect the bees mind whether they know our news or not,' she said. 'It's a very old custom that country people follow, Penny dear. You needn't bother.'

'But I'm a country person, and I like to do things like that,' said Penny. She felt certain that if she was a bee hard at work all day, she would simply love to hear any bits of news there were. 'I shall tell the bees everything, Mother!'

So Penny went solemnly out to tell the bees about Pimpernel's calf. 'Bees, I have to tell you something,' she announced. 'Pimpernel's calf is born, and it's a dear little girl-calf. But I'm sorry to say that Pimpernel isn't very well. Isn't it a pity?'

The bees hummed round her head, and Penny felt sure they were listening. 'Please bring us good luck because I've told you the news,' finished Penny.

And the funny thing was that Pimpernel was very much better that evening, and Jim couldn't think why!

'It's because I told the bees,' said Penny solemnly. 'It is, really, Jim. I shall always tell them things in future. They like it.'

'You do so, Missy, then,' said Jim, who had as great a belief as Harriet in the old country customs. 'And you look out for swarms too—maybe one of the hives will swarm in the hot weather.'

'Why do bees swarm?' asked Penny.

'Well, you see, each hive has a queen bee,' said Jim. 'But sometimes in the season there's another queen bee born, and there can't be two in a hive. So some of the bees fly off with the second queen to find a hive of their own. And you have to go after it and take it, or you'll lose half your bees!'

'Bees seem to be just as exciting as everything else,' said Penny. 'But what I'm really looking forward to is tasting their honey. Won't it be lovely to have our own?'

It *was* lovely. When the time came for the honey to be taken, there were so many pounds of it that Mother was able to put it away in store to use the whole winter through! She sent a large pot to Tammylan, who was very fond of honey. The children gave it to him the next time they visited him. They had brought him a fine lot of things, for besides honey each child had a present.

'I've brought you six of my hens' best brown eggs,' said Sheila.

'And I've brought you some of Mother's finest butter,' said Rory.

'And here's some home-made currant jelly,' said Benjy.

'And I've got you the biggest lettuce I've ever grown in my bit of garden,' said Penny. 'It has a wonderful big heart. You feel it, Tammylan.'

'As big a heart as you have, Penny!' said Tammylan, with a laugh. 'My word, I'm lucky to have four friends like you. By the way, tell your father I've heard of a bullock that wants fattening up. If he'll take it, I'll bring it along tomorrow.'

The first thing Penny did when she got home was to go to the bees and tell them about the bullock! 'Bees, there's a bullock coming!' she announced.

And when she went in, the little girl was quite certain that the bees were talking over her news as they flew to get the heather-honey from the common.

'A new bullock is coming, he's coming, yes, he's coming!' she thought she heard the bees humming. And maybe she was right!

Rory is Too Big for His Boots

That summer was a very dry one. The children revelled in the heat, and grew as brown as the old oak-apples on the trees. Haymaking time came and went. The hay was not as good as the year before, because the rain held off whilst the grass was growing. So it was not as lush as it should have been.

'Well, let's hope the rain keeps off when we cut the hay and turn it,' said the farmer. It did, and the children had a wonderful time helping with the haymaking. They were allowed a holiday from school, and they made the most of it. True helped too, galloping and scrabbling in the mown hay, sending it flying into the air.

Dopey, of course, joined the haymakers. He was now growing into a goat, and was completely mad. He still seemed to think he was a silly young kid, and played the most ridiculous tricks. He loved to spring out at the sheep and the cows, and leap around and about them so that they stared at him in the greatest amazement.

'I wouldn't mind his being such a clown,' said the farmer, 'but I do wish he wouldn't eat anything and everything. It was a mistake to give you Dopey for your birthday, Penny.'

'Oh *no*, Daddy!' said the little girl. 'I know he's silly and mad—but he does love us all.'

'Hmm!' said the farmer. 'I think I could manage quite well without Dopey's love and affection. I'm always very suspicious when that goat comes along with me.'

Penny's lambs were in the field with the other sheep now, because they ate grass. Penny always let them out when she was free from school, and they wandered around after her, baaing in their high voices. They were not allowed in the hayfield. Scamper the squirrel was allowed there, though, and he enjoyed himself very much, bounding about among the haymakers, and frisking up and down Benjy. Those days were fun, and the children were sorry when the haymaking was over.

'Daddy, will you have enough hay to feed all our cattle this winter?' asked Sheila, when she watched the haystacks being built. 'We've more cattle now, you know—and Paul Pry, the bullock, will eat an awful lot.'

The bullock had been called Paul Pry by Penny because he always appeared whenever anything was going on. He was rather a pet, very tame and very affectionate for a bullock. He simply adored joining the children when they watched such things as the ducklings going into the water for the first time, or the piglets being set free to run about the yard, squealing for joy.

'Well, we may have enough this year, but we ought to plant another field with hay next year,' said the farmer to Sheila. 'Willow Farm is growing! There's that field we haven't used yet—the one right away up there

—we might burn the bad grass and weeds in it, and then plough it up next season. The field would burn quickly enough in this weather.'

But soon after that the rain came and it was impossible to burn the rubbishy field. The children thought the idea of burning it was very exciting.

'It's a quick way of getting rid of the rubbishy grass there,' said Rory. 'I hope Daddy will do it as soon as the hot weather sets in again. Won't it be fun to set light to it?'

Rory was feeling rather big these days. He had done well on the farm that summer, because he was now very strong, and could do almost a man's work. The farmer was proud of him and praised him often. A little too often! Rory was getting 'too big for his boots,' Jim said.

'Why don't you ask Mother to buy you some new boots, Rory?' said Penny, looking at her brother's feet. 'Jim says you are getting too big for your boots—you'll get sore feet, if you're not careful.'

'You *are* a little silly, Penny!' said Rory crossly. He went out and banged the door.

'What's the matter with Rory?' asked Penny in astonishment.

'Well, don't you know what "getting too big for your boots" means?' said Sheila, with a laugh. 'It means getting vain or conceited or swollen headed—having too high an opinion of yourself!'

'Oh,' said Penny in dismay, 'what a silly I am!'

Rory had gone out into the fields. He was hailed by his father. 'Rory! I've got to go over to Headley's farm to look at some things they've got to sell. Keep an eye on things for me, will you?'

'Yes, Dad!' called back Rory, feeling all important again. He saw Mark coming along, and hoped he had heard what his father had said. Mark had. He looked rather impressed.

'It's a good thing Dad has got me to see to things for him whilst he's away here and there, isn't it?' said Rory to Mark. 'Come on. Let's look how the wheat's coming along. We'll be harvesting it soon.'

The two boys went through the fields. Mark listened to Rory talking about this crop and that crop. He was not so old as the bigger boy, and he thought Rory was really very clever and grown-up.

They came to the field that had lain waste since the farmer had taken over Willow Farm the year before. It was the one that was going to be burnt.

'This is an awful field, isn't it?' said Mark. 'It's not like Willow Farm, somehow.'

'We're going to burn it up,' said Rory. 'It's no good as it is. We must set it on fire, and then the rubbishy grass and weeds will go up in smoke, and we can put the field under the plough. Maybe next year it will be yielding a fine crop of hay, or potatoes, or something like that. Potatoes clean up a field well, you know.'

'Do they really?' said Mark, thinking that Rory knew almost as much as the farmer himself. 'I say—what fun to burn up a field? It looks about ready to burn now, doesn't it? All dry and tindery.'

'It does,' agreed Rory. He looked at the big four-acre field. He wished he could burn it then and there. It would be fun!

'You'll have to wait till your father gives orders for that, I suppose,' said Mark. 'He wouldn't allow you to start a thing like that unless he said so, would he?'

'Well—you heard what he said—I was to keep an eye on things for him,' said Rory. 'I don't see why I shouldn't burn up this field today. It looks about right for it. Which way is the wind blowing? We mustn't fire it if the wind is blowing in the wrong direction. We don't want those sheds to go up in smoke!'

The boys wetted their hands and held them out to the breeze. It seemed to be blowing the right way, away from the sheds, and towards the open country.

'Well—what about it?' said Mark, his eyes gleaming. 'Do you really dare to without your father telling you?'

'Of course,' said Rory grandly. 'I'll go and get some matches. It's easy. You just set light to a patch of grass, and then let the breeze take it over the field. We shall see the grass and everything flaring up, and by the time Daddy comes back, the field will be done.'

The two boys went to get some matches. 'What do you want them for?' asked Harriet.

'We're going to fire that rubbishy field away up above the horses' field,' said Rory.

Harriet thought that the farmer was going to be there too. She handed over some matches. 'Well, see you don't burn yourselves,' she said. 'It's easy enough to light a fire, but not so easy to put it out!'

159

'Oh, a bit of stamping soon puts out a field fire,' said Rory grandly, as if he knew everything about it. He took the matches and he and Mark set off back to the field. Penny joined them, Dopey skipping about behind her.

'Where are you going?' she asked. She jumped in excitement when she heard what they were going to do. 'I'll come with you!' she said.

So they all of them came to the field. Rory struck a match, bent down and laid the flame to a few tall dry grasses. In a trice they flared up, and the flame jumped to other grasses near by. The fire ran as if by magic!

'Look at it, look at it!' cried Penny, jumping about in excitement. 'Isn't it grand?'

It might have been grand for a minute or two—but it very soon ceased to be grand and became terrifying! Rory had started something that was impossible to stop!

An Unpleasant Adventure

'Oooh!' said Penny in surprise. 'I never thought flames could go so fast!'

Mark and Rory hadn't known that either. It was simply amazing to see the fire spread over the field. The weeds and grass were very dry from a long hot spell, and they crackled up at once. The fire grew a loud voice, and a long mane of smoky hair.

'It's alive!' said Penny, dancing about. 'It's a dragon with a mane of smoke. It's eating the field.'

Mark was excited too. He didn't dance about like Penny, but he watched the fire with shining eyes. This was much better than an ordinary bonfire.

The breeze blew a little, and the fire crackled more loudly and grew a bigger mane of smoke. Rory looked a little worried. He hadn't guessed that the flames would rush along like this. They tore over the field, leaving a blackened track behind them.

As the fire burned, the sun went in, and a pall of clouds gathered. The children hardly noticed, they were so intent on the field-fire. But then Rory saw something strange.

'Look!' he said. 'The wind must be changing! The flames are blowing the other way now.'

So they were. Instead of blowing straight down the field towards the open country, they were blowing sideways, eating up all the grass towards the east. The crackling grew louder, the smoke grew thicker.

'Rory! Won't those sheds be burnt!' cried Penny suddenly. 'Oh, Rory! Make the fire stop!'

'Stamp it out, quick!' cried Rory, and ran to where the edge of the fire began. But it was quite impossible to stamp it out. Soon the soles of their shoes were so hot that their feet felt as if they were on fire. Rory pushed Penny back. He was afraid the flames would burn her. Dopey, the kid, was the only one who seemed quite unafraid. He danced around the fire-edge, bleating at it.

'Mark! Run and tell Jim what's happened, and you, Penny, go and find Bill,' said Rory. They sped off, fear making them run even faster than usual. Mark soon found Jim, who was already staring in puzzled amazement at the stream of smoke coming from the field up the hill. In a few words he told him what had happened.

Penny found Bill and before she had half told him what had happened, he had guessed and was rushing towards the out-building where empty sacks were kept. He yelled for Harriet as he ran.

'Harriet! Come and soak these sacks. The old field is afire. Those sheds will be burnt down!'

Harriet and Fanny came tearing out in surprise. The three of them dragged the sacks down to the duck-pond and soaked them well. Then they ran as fast as they could with the heavy sacks up to the flaming field.

'Stamp it out, quick!' cried Rory.

Halfway there they met Jim rushing along with Mark. Bill threw them a couple of wet sacks.

Soon they were all in the flaming grass, beating frantically at the fire. Slap, slap, slap! Harriet, Jim, Fanny, Bill and Rory beat the wet sacks down on the flames, trying their hardest to put them out.

'I've got the fire out in this bit!' gasped Bill. 'Look up there, Jim—it's getting too near those sheds. You go there and beat it, and I'll work around behind you. We may save the sheds then.'

'The flames are running to that electric pole!' squealed Penny. 'Oh, quick; oh, quick!'

Rory and Harriet ran to the pole and tried to beat off the flames. 'Go and get some more wet sacks!' panted Harriet to Mark. 'Ours are getting dry with the heat. Oh my, oh my, who ever thought of firing this field today! With the grass as dry as it is, who knows where the fire will end!'

'Oh, it won't burn our farmhouse, will it!' cried Penny in fright.

'Come on, help me get some wet sacks,' said Mark, and pulled the frightened little girl along with him.

In half an hour's time nobody would have recognised any of the people who were beating out the flames. They were black with the smoke, they smelt terrible, and they were so hot and parched with thirst that they could hardly swallow.

Fanny gave up first. Her arms ached so badly with slapping at the flames that she could no longer lift them. She let her sack fall, and with tears rolling down her blackened cheeks, she staggered out of the smoke and sank down by the gate of the field. 'I can't slap any more,' she said. 'I can't do it any more!'

Harriet gave up next. She stood and looked at the burning field, shaking her head.

'It's no use,' she said. 'No use at all. The fire's like a mad thing, running this way and that!'

So it was. The wind had got up properly now, and blew in furious gusts that sent the flames careering now here and now there. There was no saving the field or the hedge at the top, which was already a blackened, twisted mass, all its green leaves gone.

Rory, Bill and Jim were trying to save the sheds from being burnt. Already flames licked along one shed. Jim was beating madly at them, his trousers scorched, and his feet so hot that he could hardly walk. The two men and the boy were now so tired that they, like Harriet, could hardly lift up their arms to slap their wet sacks at the flames. But still they went on valiantly, slap, slap, slap. Rory was so horrified at the damage he had caused that he was determined not to stop fighting the fire till he dropped down with tiredness.

'We can't do any more,' said Jim at last. The fire's beaten us, boys.'

'No, no, let's go on!' cried poor Rory. 'I can't let Daddy's sheds be burnt.'

'You'll have to,' said Jim. 'And those telegraph poles too. Let's hope the fire won't jump the hedge and get into the next field.'

Everyone stood and watched the hungry fire, which crackled along the edge of the first shed, shooting out little red tongues of flames at the other two huts. There was nothing to be done. Nothing could save the sheds and the poles—and maybe the next field too would soon be in flames.

Nothing? Well, only one thing. Water would put out the flames—but where was water to come from? The nearest stream was two fields away, and it wouldn't be any good trying to cart water from it to the fire.

And then Penny gave such a squeal that everyone jumped in fright, thinking that the little girl was being burnt.

'Look, oh look!' yelled Penny, pointing to the sky. 'Rain! rain!'

Everyone looked up at the black sky. Heavy drops of rain began to fall, splashing clown on the upturned, tired faces, washing patches of white in the black skins. Down and down fell the thunder-rain, while a crash suddenly sounded to the west.

'A storm!' cried Fanny. 'That will put the fire out. Oh, what a blessed mercy!'

Trembling with tiredness and relief, the exhausted little company stood there in the pouring rain, watching it put out thé hungry flames. Pitter, patter, pitter, patter, down it fell, great drops as round as coins when they splashed on the burnt ground. Everyone was soaked. Nobody cared at all. It was marvellous, wonderful, unbelievable that the rain should have come at such a moment, when everyone had given up hope!

Penny began to cry. So did Fanny. And suddenly poor Rory burst out into great sobs too. He had been so worried, so anxious—and it had all been his fault!

'Come now,' said Harriet, putting her arm comfortingly round Rory. 'It's all right. No harm's done. None at all, except that the hedge is burnt over there, and that shed got a bit of a scorching. You come along with me and Fanny, and I'll give you all something to eat and drink. Come along now.'

So everyone went along with Harriet in the pouring rain, far too tired to run. Penny went with Rory, her hand in his, so sorry for her big brother that she could not squeeze his hand hard enough. Rory's tears had made a white channel down his blackened checks and he looked very strange.

'Come now,' said Harriet, putting her arm comfortingly around Rory.

Soon they were all sitting down in the kitchen, whilst Harriet, who had not stopped to clean herself, got them something to eat and drink.

Benjy and Sheila came in to see what was happening and they stared in the utmost amazement at the sooty company. Mark laughed at their astonished faces. Everyone was feeling much better already, and the adventure was beginning to seem more exciting than unpleasant, now that it had ended better than they had hoped.

'What's happened?' said Benjy at last.

'That field atop of the hill there got fired,' said Jim. 'It's a mystery how it did.'

'I fired it,' said Rory, his face red beneath its black.

'Well—you *were* a wonderful great ninny then!' said Jim. 'What'll your father say?'

'Rory doesn't need to tell him,' said Harriet, who was sorry for the boy. 'Nobody will tell on him.'

'Harriet, of course I must tell my father,' said Rory with surprise. 'You don't suppose I'd deceive him or tell him lies, do you?'

'I should jolly well think not,' said Benjy. 'Rory isn't afraid of owning up to anything. Never has been.'

'There's Daddy's car now!' said Penny. She ran to the window and looked out, her face still black. 'Hallo, Daddy! Hallo, Mother!'

'Penny! Whatever's the matter with your face?' cried her mother. 'What *have* you been doing?'

The little girl's father and mother came to the window and looked in. They were silent with astonishment when they saw the surprising company there, all

168

eating together, and all with black faces and scorched clothes.

Rory stood up. 'I'll tell you, Daddy,' he said, and he went out of the kitchen, and met his father at the hall door. They went together into the little study.

'I fired the top field,' said Rory. 'I—I thought it would be all right.'

'Why did you do that?' asked his father.

'Well—I thought it looked all right for firing,' said Rory. 'I know I shouldn't have done it without your permission. I—I—think I got too big for my boots, as Penny says.'

'Yes—I think you did,' said his father. 'But you seem to have gone back to your right size again, my boy. I suppose the field took fire and the sheds went up in smoke too?'

'They nearly did,' said Rory honestly. 'But the rain came just in time and saved them, Dad. There's not much damage done, except that one hedge is burnt.'

'That's lucky then,' said his father. 'We might have had a serious loss. You must never start a grass-fire unless you've got a whole lot of helpers round to beat it out when necessary, Rory. It runs like magic.'

'I know,' said Rory. 'It was dreadful. I was awfully scared. All the others came to help, and that's why we're so black and scorched. I do blame myself terribly.'

'Quite right too,' said his father. 'You were very much to blame. But I was to blame too! I've forgotten you were only a lad of fourteen, and I've made you think yourself a man. Well—you're not. You're just a lad yet—and a very good one too! But you've behaved like a man tonight, in coming to me like this, and telling me everything. Now go and wash your face.'

Rory went off, feeling his father's hand clapping him affectionately on the shoulder. 'Dad's splendid!' he thought. 'I shan't behave like that again—getting too big for my boots, and thinking I know everything!'

Everyone went to clean themselves and to put on fresh clothes, for they smelt of smoke. As Penny was just putting on a clean jersey, she gave a scream that made Sheila jump.

'Oh! Oh! What's happened to Dopey, do you think? Did he get burnt? I've not seen him for ages!' Nobody had seen Dopey. Penny dragged on her jersey, shouting out that she must go and find him, she must, she must!

She tore out into the farmyard, and there she saw True barking frantically at a peculiar little object in the middle of the yard. It was quite black and very miserable. Penny stood and stared at it. Then she gave a yell, ran to it, and hugged it.

'*Dopey*! You're all black, just like I was! Darling Dopey, you're not burnt, are you?'

Dopey wasn't. Silly as he was, he wasn't quite so silly as that! He snuggled against Penny contentedly.

'Penny!' said Mother, appearing at the door. 'Penny! What is the sense of putting on perfectly clean things and then hugging a black and sooty goat? I think you must be just as mad as Dopey!'

Ups and Downs

The first year that the family had been at Willow Farm had been so successful that everyone had rather got into the way of thinking that farming was really quite easy. But the second year showed them that a farm had its 'downs' as well as its 'ups,' as Penny put it.

'We had all "ups" last year,' she said. 'This year we've had some "downs"—like when Daddy bought that mad bull and lost half the price he paid for it—and when Rory fired the field and we nearly lost the sheds.'

'And when Mark left the gate open and we hunted for hours for the lost horses, and Daddy had to do without them for a while,' said Sheila. 'And this year the hay isn't so good.'

'But the corn is even better,' said Rory. 'So that's an "up," isn't it? And, Sheila, your hens and ducks have done marvellously again this year, you know.'

'Except that I lost a whole brood of darling little ducklings to the rats,' said Sheila sorrowfully. That had been a great blow to her and Fanny. Twelve little yellow and black ducklings had disappeared in two nights.

Jim had said that it was rats, and he had set traps for them. But the rats were too cunning for the traps, and not one had been caught.

Then Bill had brought along a white ferret, a clever little creature that slipped like lightning down a rat-hole to chase the rats. The men had been waiting at other rat-holes, watching for the scared rats to come out. They had killed a good many and were satisfied.

'Ah, rats are no good at all,' said Bill. 'Most creatures are some good—but rats are just the worst creatures ever made. They aren't even kind to their own sort. And they're too clever for anything.'

Sheila had been glad to know that the rats around the duck-pond had been killed. She loved all her baby birds and had cried bitterly when she knew so many had been eaten by the hungry rats. But in spite of the damage done to her little flock of birds, she had done extremely well with her eggs and chicks and ducklings. Mother said she was an excellent little business woman already.

'Fanny's a great help, Mother,' Sheila said, when her mother praised her. 'I think we ought to raise her wages, don't you? The rise could come out of our egg-profits.'

So Fanny's wages were raised, and the girl was proud and pleased. She spent her first week's rise on little presents for her many brothers and sisters. That was just like Fanny!

All the children on the farm loved the animals, both wild and tame, that lived on and around it—with the exception of the rats, of course. But the farmer used to get cross when he heard Penny or Benjy talking with delight about the rabbits on the hillside!

'Rabbits!' he would say in disgust. 'Stop raving about them, do! They've done more damage to my farm this year than anything else. I'd like to shoot the lot.'

172

'Oh *no*, Daddy!' Penny cried every time. 'Oh no! You can't shoot those dear little long-eared creatures with their funny little white bobtails.'

'Well, if they eat any more of my seedlings in Long Meadow, I'll shoot the whole bunch!' threatened her father.

Penny went solemnly to the hillside to warn the rabbits. Rory heard her talking to them. He was mending a gap in the hedge near by, and Penny didn't see him.

'Rabbits,' said Penny, in her clear voice, 'you'll be shot and killed if you don't leave my Daddy's fields alone. Now, you've got plenty of grass to eat up here, and I'll bring you lettuce leaves for a treat when I can. So do leave Daddy's seedlings alone—*especially* the vetch that is growing in Long Meadow. It's going to feed the cattle, and it's very important.'

Rory laughed quietly to himself. Penny was so funny. He watched his little sister skip down the hillside as lightly as a lamb. He hoped that the rabbits would take notice of what she said, for he knew she would be very upset if they were shot.

But alas! The rabbits took no notice at all. In fact, it seemed as if they made up their minds to do as much damage as possible, as soon as they could. The very next morning the farmer came in to breakfast looking as black as thunder. Rory looked at him in surprise.

'What's up, Dad?' he asked.

'The rabbits have eaten nearly every scrap of that big field of vetch seedlings,' said his father. 'That's a serious loss. I doubt if we can plant any more seed. It's too late in the year. I'll have to get a few guns together and do some shooting.'

Penny didn't say anything, nor did Benjy. But they both looked sad. After breakfast they went to have a look at the field. Their father was right. The vetch was almost completely spoilt, for the rabbits had eaten it right down to the ground.

'Well—you can't expect Daddy to put up with *that*,' said Benjy. 'I wonder when the rabbits will be shot.'

When the next Saturday came Daddy announced that he and three others were going to shoot the rabbits all over the farm. Penny burst into tears.

'Take Penny to see Tammylan today,' said Mother quickly to Benjy. So she and Benjy went over the hill to visit the wild man. They told him about the rabbits. Even as they told him there came the first crack of a distant gun.

'One poor little rabbit dead, never to run down the hillside any more,' said Penny with a sob.

'Penny, dear, don't take things so much to heart,' said Tammylan. 'Your father is a farmer and has to grow food for you and for his farm friends. He would be foolish to allow all his work to be wasted because he wouldn't fight his enemies the rats, the rabbits and many kinds of insects. What would you say if he said to you, 'Penny, I'm sorry I've no food for you, because the rabbits and rats came and took it and I hadn't the heart to stop them?'

'I'd think he was silly,' said Penny, drying her eyes, and Benjy nodded too.

174

*'The rabbits have eaten nearly every scrap of that big field
of vetch seedlings,' said his father.*

'Yes, you would,' said Tammylan. 'But he isn't silly, so he is taking the quickest and kindest way of fighting his enemies. Now cheer up, and come and see my latest friend—a water-vole who will eat out of my hand!'

Penny said no more about rabbits to her father after that. She even ate rabbit-pie at dinner the next day. After all, you had to be sensible, as well as kind-hearted.

Another time the farmer complained that a whole field of potatoes had been spoilt by the pheasants that came walking among them, devouring them by the hundred. Benjy pricked up his ears at this.

'Rory, I've got an idea,' he said. 'Couldn't we train True to run round Daddy's fields and scare away the pheasants when they fly down? I'm sure we could. Do let me try to teach him.'

Rory thought it *was* a good idea—but he didn't want Benjy to do the teaching. He said he would do it himself.

'I dare say you could teach him more quickly,' he said, 'because you really are a wizard with animals—but he's my dog, and I'd rather do it, thank you, Benjy.'

So Rory began to teach True to scare off the pheasants and other birds that flew down to his father's fields. The dog, who now understood almost every word that Rory said to him, soon knew what he wanted. In a week or two, not a pheasant dared to fly down on to a field if True was anywhere about! The farmer was surprised and pleased.

'We'll buy you a new collar,' he said to True. 'You're as good as any of the children.'

'True is one of our "ups," isn't he?' said Rory proudly. True wagged his tail. He didn't know what an 'up' was, but he felt sure it was something good.

'And Dopey is one of our "downs" ', said Sheila.

Penny protested at once. 'He isn't, he isn't. Why do you say that?'

'Only because he went and butted one of my coops over, let out the hen and her chicks, and then chased the poor old hen into the pond,' said Sheila.

'And yesterday he got hold of one of the piglets by its curly tail and wouldn't let go,' said Benjy. 'The pig squealed the place down. I do think it's time Dopey had a scolding again, Penny. Scamper never does anything like that. He's always perfectly good.'

'Well—I don't like creatures that are always perfectly good,' said Penny. 'I prefer Dopey. Anyway, he'll soon be a proper goat, and then Jim says he'll have to go and live in the field with the cows. I *shall* miss him.'

'He'll be a jolly good miss, that's all I can say,' said Rory. 'How I shall look forward to missing him!'

Happy Days

Mark came to spend part of his summer holidays at Willow Farm. Since the adventure of the lost horses he had been much more careful, and was now almost as responsible as the farm children. He always adored staying at the farm, and loved all the animals as much as they did.

'You know, even when there's nothing at all happening, it's lovely to be on a farm,' he told Rory. 'It's exciting, of course, when you buy a new bull, or make the hay, or harvest the corn—but even an ordinary peaceful day is lovely, I think.'

It was. The bees hummed loudly as they went to and from the hive. The children liked to think of the golden honey being stored there. Benjy had become extremely good at handling the bees, and his father had made him responsible for them. They did not sting him at all. Rory had been stung once, and Mark twice, but nobody else.

The humming of the bees, the baaing of the sheep, the cluck of the hens, and the quack of the ducks sounded all day long at the farm. Everyone was used to the noise, and hardly noticed it except when they left the farm to go to the town—and then they missed all the familiar sounds very much.

Then there were the shouts of the men at work, coming suddenly on the air—an unexpected whinny from a waiting horse, and a stamp of hoofs—a mooing from a cow, and a squeal from a pig. Sometimes there was the clatter of a pail, or the sound of children's running feet, coming home from school. It was a happy farm, with everyone doing his work well, and everyone helping the other.

Mother used to laugh at the way the animals and birds came to the house. This always astonished visitors too. The hens came regularly to the kitchen door, and were as regularly shooed away by Harriet. Mr By-Himself sometimes did a bit of shooing when he felt like it, but the hens did not really fear him. If there was no one in the kitchen they would walk right in and peck about.

Sometimes they would go into the house by the open French windows of the sitting-room, clucking importantly. If Mother had visitors, the visitors would say 'How sweet!' But Mother didn't think so, and out would go the hens at top speed.

Once one of the ducks brought all her little yellow ducklings into the house, much to Penny's delight. 'Mother, the duck-pond is almost dried up, and I expect the duck wants to find the bath for her ducks to swim on,' said Penny. 'Oh, Mother, do let me run the bath full for them, *please!*'

But to Penny's great disappointment she was not allowed to, and the duck had to take her string of youngsters to the stream, where they all bobbed and swam to their hearts' content.

The big cart-horses often came into the farmyard and stood there whilst Jim or Bill went to have a word with Harriet. If they thought Penny was anywhere about they would wander to the house, and put their heads in at the door or the window. It always gave the children a real thrill to look up and see the big brown head looking in, the large eyes asking silently for a lump of sugar.

'Oh! Darling! Wait a minute, wait a minute! I'll just get you some sugar!' Penny would say, dropping her knitting or her book at once. And the patient horse would stand there, blinking long-lashed eyes, his head almost filling the window. Once Captain even went into the hall, and knocked over the umbrella stand with such a crash that he backed out hastily, stepping on the foot-scraper and smashing it to bits.

'Don't be cross with him, Mother!' begged Benjy when he heard about it. Benjy had been in bed with a cold at the time. 'Mother, I'm sure Captain came to look for me. He must have wondered why I didn't groom him. I'll pay for a new foot-scraper.'

'Oh, I think I can manage that!' said Mother, with a laugh. 'So long as you hurry up and get better, Benjy. I don't want cows and horses and sheep tramping up the stairs all day long to ask how you are!'

The sheep never came over to the house, except Hoppitty and Jumpity, who had been brought up by hand. They ran in and out continually, though Mother always chased them away. She did her best to make the children keep the doors shut, but except for Mark, who always shut gates and doors behind him, wherever he was, the farm children left the house-doors open. Penny

It was a happy farm.

secretly loved the animals coming into the house, and one of her happiest memories was going into the sitting-room one day and finding Hoppitty, Jumpity and Dopey lying asleep on the old rug in front of the fire! The little girl had lain down beside them and gone to sleep too.

'Well, what a heap of tired creatures!' Harriet had said, when she came in to lay the tea. 'I'm surprised you don't give them a place in your bed, that I am, Penny!'

Penny had thought that was a splendid idea, but Mother had said 'no' so decidedly that Penny hadn't even bothered to ask twice.

'Willow Farm is such a friendly place,' Mark said, dozens of times. 'Whenever I come I feel as if the hens cluck "Good morning!" to me, and the ducks say "Hallo!" The horses say "What, you again!" and the pigs squeal out, "Here's Mark! Here's Mark!" And the …'

'The children say, "Oh, what a bore—here's that tiresome boy again!" ' said Rory with a grin.

Even Paul Pry, the new bullock, took to being friendly enough to pay a call at the house. He usually went to the kitchen, because, for some reason or other, he had taken a great fancy to Harriet. He would arrive there, and stand at the door, his big head lowered, looking anxiously into the kitchen, waiting for Harriet to appear. He only once attempted to go right into the kitchen, much to the astonishment and fright of Mr By-Himself, who was fast asleep on a chair. He awoke to find Paul Pry standing over him, breathing hard.

Mr By-Himself leapt straight into the air, and spat so loudly that the bullock was scared. He backed hastily and knocked over the kitchen table. It was full of saucepans and pans that Fanny was to clean. They went over with a crash that brought Fanny and Harriet and Mother out of the dairy at a run.

'Paul Pry!' exclaimed Harriet in wrath. 'Who told *you* to come into the kitchen then? Knocking over my table like that! Out you go, and don't you dare to come and see me again!'

And out went the poor bullock as meekly as a lamb, sad that Harriet was cross with him. But he was back again two days later, staring in at the door for his beloved Harriet.

'Well, there's one thing,' said the farmer, with a laugh, 'if ever Paul Pry goes mad like Stamper, we shall know who can deal with him. Harriet would put him right with a shoo from her broom. To see her chase the bullock away is the funniest sight in the world. And yet I think she is very fond of him.'

That was the nice part of Willow Farm. Men, women, children and animals were all fond of one another. The creatures trusted their masters and mistresses, and never expected or got anything but kindness and understanding. Nobody slacked, nobody shirked his work, everyone did his bit.

And so Willow Farm, in spite of more 'downs' than 'ups' that second year, prospered and did well. New cow-sheds were built—beautiful places, airy and clean. New machinery was bought and admired, put to use and then cleaned and stored until next time. New animals were born, named and loved. New fields were cleaned, ploughed and sown.

'It's a family farm,' said Rory happily. 'We've all got our jobs and we try to do them well. Daddy, aren't you glad you gave up your London work and came here, to Willow Farm?'

'Very glad,' said his father. 'I've seen you all grow healthy and strong. I've seen you doing work that matters. I've watched you learning good lessons as you handle the animals and help to till the soil. You've had to use your muscles and you've had to use your brains. You've grown up complete and whole, with no nonsense in you. I'm proud of you all.'

'I hope we'll never have to leave,' said Benjy. 'I couldn't bear to have to live in town now, Daddy. I hope Willow Farm never fails.'

'There's no reason why it should,' said the farmer. 'After all, ours is a mixed farm, and there is no waste anywhere.'

'That's true,' said Rory. 'We grow corn and it feeds the hens we want to keep. We grow fodder and it feeds the cows whose milk we need. They give us cream and butter and cheese, and the skim milk goes to the pigs and the calves. The hens in turn give us eggs.'

'It's a pity we can't grow our own clothes,' said Penny. 'Then we could almost live on the farm without buying a single thing.'

'Well, the second year is over,' said the farmer. 'We've made mistakes, and sometimes had misfortune and bad luck—but here we all are, happy and healthy, with the farm growing bigger than ever. Good luck to Willow Farm!'

And that is what we all say too—good luck to Willow Farm. We will peep in at the window before we say good-bye and see them all sitting round the fire there, one wintry Sunday afternoon.

There is Rory, big and strong, with Sheila beside him, adding up her egg-book. And there is Benjy, nursing Scamper as usual. And there, on the rug, is little Penny, who has been allowed to have Dopey in for a treat. He is trying to bite True's ears, but the dog will not let him.

Outside there is the tread of feet coming to the door. The sound makes Penny jump up and go to the window. 'It's Mark—and Tammylan! They've come to tea. Hallo, Mark! Hallo, Tammylan! Wait a minute till I open the door!'

She flies to open it, and it would be nice if we could slip in too. But the door is closed and we are left outside alone.

Not quite alone! A hen pecks at our legs, and a horse whinnies softly from the stables. Davey's sheep baa in their folds and Rascal barks in the distance. The first star shines out in the sky and we must go.

Good-bye, Willow Farm! May you always be the same friendly place that we know and love so well.

The End

Other titles in this series: